ACCLAIM FOR
LOVED, LOST, FOUND

These are inspiring stories of real people that need to be read not only once but over and over again, so they can be fully appreciated. They are, in other words, stories worth meditating on. To quote Blessed John Paul II, people — like these described here— live, as we all do, in a world that is indeed too often "marked by terrible tragedies," but they have also heard in the message of Divine Mercy "the appropriate and incisive answer" that God offers "to the questions and expectations of human beings in our time." This book demonstrates in the most effective way possible — through the lives of people like us — how the "restorative tide of God's merciful love continues to spread over the men and women of our time."

— MSGR. JAMES LISANTE
Pastor, author, radio/TV host and commentator

Pope Paul VI once said that we listen more willingly today to witnesses than to teachers, and that if we do listen to teachers, it is because they are witnesses. Felix Carroll has given us 17 witnesses in this beautiful book who teach us through the stories of their lives that God's mercy is available to us as well. I highly recommend this book, which is hard to put down. Felix has done a wonderful job of showing us that God is real, that He is close to us, and that He is doing great things in people's lives. We learn what is possible if we open our hearts and trust in God's merciful love.

— FR. JOSEPH G. ROESCH, MIC
Vicar General of the Marian Fathers of
the Immaculate Conception

signature

Loved, Lost,
FOUND

17 Divine Mercy Conversions

Felix Carroll

MARIAN PRESS
STOCKBRIDGE MA 01263

2013

Available from:
Marian Helpers Center
Stockbridge, MA 01263

Prayerline: 1-800-804-3823
Orderline: 1-800-462-7426
Website: www.marian.org

Imprimi Potest:
Very Rev. Kazimierz Chwalek, MIC
Provincial Superior
The Blessed Virgin Mary, Mother of Mercy Province
February 2, 2013

Library of Congress Catalog Number: 2013932409
ISBN: 978-159614-274-9

Cover Art: copyright © Marian Fathers of the Immaculate
Conception of the B.V.M.

Design of Cover and Pages: Kathy Szpak

Editing and Proofreading: David Came and Andrew Leeco

For texts from the English Edition of
Diary of St. Maria Faustina Kowalska

Nihil Obstat:
Lector Officialis
Most Rev. George H. Pearce, SNM

Imprimatur:
Most Rev. Joseph F. Maguire
Bishop of Springfield, Mass.
January 29, 1988

The NIHIL OBSTAT and IMPRIMATUR are a declaration that a book or pamphlet
is considered to be free from doctrinal or moral error. It is not implied that those who
have granted the NIHIL OBSTAT and IMPRIMATUR agree with the contents,
opinions, or statements expressed.

Printed in the United States of America

JESUS TO ST. FAUSTINA
AND ALL OF US:

The greater the sinner, the greater
the right he has to My mercy.

— *Diary of St. Faustina, 723*

*To Dr. Bryan Thatcher,
the nicest guy I know.*

CONTENTS

ACKNOWLEDGMENTS

First and foremost, I'm indebted to David Came, executive editor of *Marian Helper* magazine and Marian Press. This book was his idea, and he served as its editor. Dave: Your talent, friendship, and spiritual witness over the years have been instrumental to me in my work and spiritual life.

The Very Rev. Fr. Kazimierz Chwalek, MIC, provincial superior of the Blessed Virgin Mary, Mother of Mercy Province: for all of your support.

Father Seraphim Michalenko, MIC: for introducing me to St. Faustina and to Silvano Toso, one of the prison inmates featured in this book.

Father Michael Gaitley, MIC, director of the Association of Marian Helpers: I've never met anyone who works harder.

Brother Fred Wells, MIC: for the bread, the songs, and your Virginia wisdom.

Father Martin Rzeszutek, MIC: for your "humility, humility, humility."

Father Richard Drabik, MIC: for all of your insights in matters grammatical and theological.

Father Michael Callea, MIC: I guess we're not supposed to have "favorite priests." Still, you're my favorite priest.

All the employees of the Marian Helpers Center. Special thanks to Terry Peloquin, Kathy Szpak, Robin Parow, Dan Valenti, Bill Popp (a gentleman among gentlemen), Sarah Chichester, Andy Leeco, Kevin Dougherty, John Foster, and everyone on the Divine Mercy Intercessory Prayerline.

Marian Helpers, both alive and deceased: Your prayers have helped save countless souls.

William and Kathleen Roesch, and Frank and Angie Rizzo: models for the Sacrament of Marriage. I've been meaning to tell you that.

Kathleen Ervin: No one is more thoughtful.

Dr. Robert Stackpole, STD, of the John Paul II Institute of Divine Mercy: You'd be the first to acknowledge you don't have all the answers, but allow me to be the first to acknowledge you certainly have a lot of them.

My parents, brothers, and sister: We have our faults, but we have our humor.

Thanks to my wife, Cara, and son, Henry: for *everything*. You made me what I am today (the good qualities, that is). And sorry how I so greatly underestimated the time it would take me to write this book. Cara: We really should get a babysitter.

Saint Maria Faustina: I'd like to think you co-wrote this.

PREFACE

Spoiler alert: The 17 people we profile here all find God in the end. So the question is, why read stories if you already know their ending? The answer is simple: Because you *don't know the beginning.*

Between points A and B — between a person being "lost" and then "found" — are infinite permutations, boundless possibilities through the gift and subsequent hazards of free will, that only go to show how much God loves us. Probably the best way to appreciate His boundless love is to take a look at the facts — the brokenness and despair between points A to B — that lead to the conversion of hearts. In other words, we offer this book to illustrate that no matter what we've done, no matter how much we've made a mess of our lives, no matter how we've abandoned Him in our fruitless searches for salvation in the material things of this world, God will embrace us when we turn to Him with repentance, trust, and love. He will embrace us just as the father embraces the wayward son who returns home in the parable of the Prodigal Son (see Lk 15:11-32).

In that light, consider this book a pilgrimage in reverse — from the foot of the cross backwards and into the broken lives lived far away from Him. In fact, "pilgrimage" seems the most appropriate term because this book was written at a popular pilgrimage destination: Eden Hill, home of the National Shrine of The Divine Mercy, in Stockbridge, Massachusetts, which is administered by the Marian Fathers of the Immaculate Conception. Indeed, this book is inspired by my experiences during the past eight years here, meeting and writing about many of these pilgrims in my role as a member of the Marians' Editorial Department. They all have stories to tell of their extraordinary journeys from A to B. Many of them visit the Shrine in order to encounter God, to learn more about *who He is*, and to give Him thanks for the graces He's given them. Certainly, the work of salvation is the greatest story to be told. To that point, what my colleagues and I here on Eden Hill have discovered is that the most popular stories we publish for our magazine, *Marian Helper*, or post on our websites, thedivinemercy.org and marian.org, are not of the deep theological variety (though such work is important). Rather, they are the stories of everyday people who discover God's extraordinary mercy.

This book features 17 such people. We met them either through their connections with the Shrine and the Marian Fathers or through people with a connection to the Shrine and the Marian Fathers. For readers of *Marian Helper*, the names Scot Bateman, Bryan Thatcher, Valdemar Welz, Fred Berretta, and Kellie Ross may sound familiar. We've previously written about them in some fashion. But in this book, we take the opportunity to get to know them better — in most cases to join them in their ministries on the road and/or to spend time with them in their hometowns. We learn a lot more about them than we knew before. But you probably have never heard of most of the people we feature here. I wrote their stories in 2012-13 after quite a bit of traveling: to Texas, Florida, Virginia, Washington, D.C., New Mexico, New York, Ohio, Illinois, and points throughout my home state of Massachusetts. The story on Kellie Ross is based on my time with her in Africa, Virginia, and Washington, D.C., during a several-year span beginning in 2009.

The people you will read about include two prisoners, a blind man, a former "workaholic," an unfaithful husband, a former cult member, a rape victim, a former abortionist, a survivor of a plane crash, and a former professional football player, among others.

Appropriately, the book begins with Maureen Digan whose miracle healing in 1981 led to the beatification of Sr. Maria Faustina Kowalska. As to Sr. Faustina (now a saint), her revelations in the 1930s — what we know today as the message of Divine Mercy — play a major role in each one of these conversion stories. Through St. Faustina, Jesus reiterates for our times the Gospel message that He is Love and Mercy itself, and that He calls us to turn to Him in trust, receive His mercy, and extend His mercy to others. In case you have never read St. Faustina's *Diary*, I highly recommend it.

I humbly thank the 17 people featured in the following pages. They opened their homes to me, and they opened their hearts. Some shared intimate, often painful, experiences — things they hadn't talked about before to anyone. They did so courageously and prayerfully with the single hope that other souls could be saved through their witness. I am honored to call these 17 people my new friends. I am honored to tell their stories.

These are love stories.

Felix Carroll
February 2013
Stockbridge, Massachusetts

Felix Carroll

CHAPTER 1

Maureen Digan

Life after the Miracle

Jesus to St. Faustina:

You will prepare the world for My final coming.

— Diary of St. Faustina, 429

When you sit at their dining room table and the earth starts shaking, which it does from time to time, Bob and Maureen Digan don't even blink. The windows rattle. The floor trembles. They're used to it.

You would be excused for thinking to yourself: *So this is how life goes when you experience a miracle that leads to the beatification of a Polish mystic whose revelations have changed the world: The earth itself must continually adjust under the weight of it all.*

Seeing my perplexed expression during a visit, Bob and Maureen calmly explain that the shaking is not the manifestation of a supernatural act of God, but rather from explosives at the nearby marble quarry. Indeed, the only thing that seems out of the ordinary about Bob and Maureen Digan is how ordinary they seem today. They live quietly in a modest house in western Massachusetts, on a working-class street, in a tiny, old mill town. They drive a minivan. And yet their lives interlock at the very epicenter of the mission given to St. Maria Faustina (1905-1938), the "Apostle of the Divine Mercy," whom the Lord entrusted to "prepare the world for My final coming" (*Diary of St. Faustina*, 429). March 28, 2013, marked 32 years since Bob and Maureen experienced a miracle through the intercession of this humble Polish nun. Thirty-two years, and Bob is still "Bob," the guileless, gentle, self-deprecating Marine veteran with the thick East Boston accent and unflappable faith. Maureen is still "Maureen," with the weariness and wisdom of the world, whose no-nonsense manner extends to most things, even her own maladies, even her own miracle.

She's still Maureen, wheelchair-bound, who quite reluctantly found herself before the tomb of Faustina in Poland on the evening of March 28, 1981, and who said, "Okay, Faustina, I came a long way, now *do* something." Maureen was healed on the spot from Melroy's lymphedema, an incurable disease.

She's matter-of-fact about most matters, except Bobby, their boy who died in 1991. When the conversation turns to Bobby's difficult life and blessed death, it only goes to show how

Bob and Maureen are still *of* this world. They still struggle. They still suffer. Like everyone else.

"Life goes on," says Bob, who's sipping coffee from a mug. The mug is emblazoned with the words, "The Man, The Myth, The Legend" — not far from the mark, any of it. Bob Digan's life *does* seem the stuff of legend. Despite the fact he was raised in a highly dysfunctional family, he remained steadfast in his Catholic faith. Despite the fact he had only just laid eyes on her for the first time, he vowed then and there, back in 1959, that he would someday marry Maureen. Despite the fact she spent most of her teen years in a hospital bed and eventually had to have her right leg amputated, his love for her only grew. And this was just the beginning.

Despite the fact all would soon appear bleak beyond measure for him and his young family, Bob trusted in God. His trust would eventually give proof to St. Faustina's promise before her death of "boundless action" for the sake of poor souls who turn with trust to God's mercy.

✝

It wasn't love at first sight for Maureen. She's one to weigh the facts. God Himself would have to wait. So would Bob Digan.

"Dixie Digan" was what his buddies called him. His neighborhood bordered Boston's Logan Airport, with its eternal clamor of jet engines and furious movement of humanity. In this atmosphere, to seize a quiet fixed point could be viewed nearly as an act of rebellion. His quiet fixed point became the Catholic faith — his parish church and his prayer life.

Maureen Cahill, the child of devout Catholics who emigrated from Ireland, grew up in Brookline, just west of the Boston city limits. Her oldest brother, a priest, served Bob's parish. Maureen was visiting her brother one day, and that's how she and Bob met.

"I was playing drums for the drill team, practicing in the church hall," Bob recalls. "I saw five girls way at the end walking in. And I zeroed in on Maureen. I didn't know her. Never met her. And I stopped drumming and said to the kid next to me: 'Buddy, I don't understand this, but someday I'm going to marry that girl.'"

He was 15 at the time. Maureen was still in grammar school. They met that night outside the church. Maureen says it took a few meetings for it to turn into "puppy love" for her.

As Maureen began her sophomore year in high school, she learned she had lymphedema, a condition in which excess fluid collects in tissue and causes swelling. In her case, the swelling was in the legs. Her life would forever change. She would spend long stretches in the hospital. She would undergo more than 50 operations. She would lose her school friends and endure countless disappointments.

But Bob was there for her, in a Marine uniform by then. He had become her very own unflustered fixed point.

"I had pushed God pretty much out of my life," says Maureen. "I didn't go to confession. I would not go to Mass. I would wonder why the other kids were so happy, and I'm not. Everything was God's fault." Even as her parents would tell her, "It's okay. Trust in God. God is good. He'll have something special planned for you." Maureen would think, "Thanks, but no thanks."

She fell into depression. Then, she developed seizures. Her doctors put her on anticonvulsants, anti-depressants, and heavy seizure medications. She became addicted to these prescription drugs. "I began to want to stay in the hospital," she says, "because I felt safe there, and I didn't care if I went home or not because I no longer wanted to face reality."

Bob would come up from Camp Lejeune, North Carolina, on weekends, an 18-hour drive and then another 18-hour drive back on Sunday. When he was eventually stationed in Maine, his weekend visits continued. During that time, some of the nurses tried to influence Maureen. "Let him go," they'd tell her. "Give him his freedom." They made her feel guilty that Bob was only visiting her out of sympathy. She'd begun to think, "He's a good Catholic, and he doesn't want to hurt me." Though she loved him, she broke up with him — "for his sake." She blamed God. And the disappointments continued. She had to have her right leg amputated above the knee. Then, it had to be amputated to the hip.

Bob walked in to her hospital room one day, a motorcycle helmet in one hand and a rose in the other. He bowed his head and said, "You know, there's a girl I'd like to marry, but I'm afraid to ask her because I'm afraid she might say no." Never thinking he was referring to herself, Maureen said, "Well, why don't you ask her, Bob? All she can do is say no."

"Okay," he said, "will you marry me?"

Before the wedding, a meeting was demanded by Maureen's doctor to inform both — but especially Bob — of Maureen's condition. She would never improve from the incurable lymphedema, the doctor said, and she might not ever be able to have children.

"It's okay, whatever God sends, we accept," Bob said. "Whatever God doesn't send, we accept."

Maureen wanted a house full of children. So did Bob.

They wed on June 6, 1970. Maureen strapped on a prosthetic leg for the first and last time. It was painful. But it enabled her to walk down the aisle and to dance to the song "Daddy's Little Girl."

✝

She got pregnant a couple months into the marriage. For the first time in years, she tried to trust God, to let Him into her heart. The baby died before it came to term. She blamed God.

"I don't know how Bob stayed so faithful and never complained," she says. "He kept trusting in God."

She got pregnant again. She tried to trust again. Bobby was born March 23, 1973.

For the first time in her life, she required no mountain of evidence to determine whether to make an emotional investment. Unlike her love for God, it wouldn't require a miracle. Unlike her love for Bob, it wouldn't require his persistence. She loved little Bobby the moment she set her eyes on him.

Still, the facts were these: He had brain damage. At 21 months, he had his first grand mal seizure, characterized by loss of consciousness and violent convulsions. From there, his health was like a runaway train downhill. Eventually, he lost his ability to walk and to talk. Some days, his seizures occurred around the clock. On his sixth birthday, he was admitted at the hospital weighing 35 pounds. He was discharged five-and-a-half months later, weighing 18 pounds and being fed through a tube. He was not expected to live for long.

Meanwhile, Maureen's lymphedema worsened in her left leg.

Bob's family was falling apart.

"We had no social life. No life," Bob recalls. "I said to myself, 'What's going on here? You have two innocent people here, and they're suffering like that. Why?'"

Occasionally, they would have a reprieve from the pain. Bob would pack Maureen and little Bobby into the car and drive them to nearby Needham, Massachusetts, where they would watch the trains go by. He'd take them to have ice cream. But, for the most part, they were prisoners in their own home, or prisoners in a hospital room.

"All the while," says Bob, "I felt God must be calling us for something. I felt He had a plan for us."

Yes, God certainly did.

✝

It was 1979, a year after the Church lifted its 20-year ban on Faustina's writings — a ban the Polish nun herself prophesied, caused by faulty translations of her writings.

Bob Digan knew nothing about Divine Mercy. But one day, a flyer arrived in the mail that advertised a film in nearby Cambridge on the topic of Divine Mercy and Sr. Faustina. He felt pulled to go see it. So one evening, while some family members kept his sick wife and child company, Bob headed off across Boston's Charles River and into Cambridge.

He recalls the film. It was produced in the United States before the ban. It was of poor quality. The film kept jamming up in the projector. Nonetheless, says Bob, the message came through loud and clear of the prophetic revelations given to the world by God through this Polish nun to proclaim the heart of the Gospels in a way especially suited to meet the needs of our era.

For Bob, something just clicked.

"I can still see him walking through the living room door that evening," says Maureen. "He had a smile on his face. He was saying, 'Isn't the name Faustina beautiful?' I remember looking at him and saying, 'It's ugly.'"

Maureen sighs. She's still a little ashamed of how bitter she had become at that point. But her bitterness could certainly be excused.

Even Bob, one evening, found himself so physically, psychologically, and spiritually drained, he literally crawled across the living room floor toward the Bible. He was crying. He said, "Lord, speak to me." He opened the Bible and pointed randomly. His finger landed on the words, "Your sins are forgiven."

Something clicked again. *Divine Mercy. God loves us. Trust. Pray. Do not be afraid.*

"God illuminated my mind with what the theologians would call an intellectual vision," Bob says. "You don't see anything; you just know."

Know what, exactly?

That would soon be revealed. Acting on impulse, he packed up his family and drove three hours west to Stockbridge, Massachusetts, the North American home of the Marian Fathers of the Immaculate Conception. He had never been to Stockbridge before. He had never met a Marian. All he knew is that he had to take his family there because he had found out the Marians were official promoters of Faustina and her Divine Mercy revelations, beginning three years after Faustina's death.

Bob parked the car by the chapel — known today as the National Shrine of The Divine Mercy. He went in and asked to see Fr. Seraphim Michalenko, MIC, the vice-postulator for Sr. Faustina's beatification cause. Bob didn't prepare Maureen for what he was about to say.

Once seated in Fr. Seraphim's office, Bob let it out. He said he had received a "collect call" from God to bring his family to Poland.

"I understood that I was to take my family to Poland, so that God's mercy then could burst forth throughout the world through Sr. Faustina," Bob explains. "And as a favor for making that trip, God would heal not one, but both Maureen and Bobby."

So, he invited Fr. Seraphim. "We want you to witness the miracle," Bob told him. Both Maureen's and Fr. Seraphim's jaws dropped.

Father Seraphim was intrigued.

Maureen was alarmed.

"He never mentioned it to me — the whole three-hour trip there," Maureen recalls. "I thought, 'Oh, my Good Lord! My Rock of Gibraltar is crumbling! Bob's becoming a religious nut. He was the only solid one, and now he's falling apart!"

"This wasn't wishful thinking," Bob recalls. "I *knew*. I was *convinced*."

With permission secured from his provincial superior, Fr. Seraphim was ready to go. And with permission secured from her doctors, Maureen was, too. Actually, she didn't want to go. She finally agreed, for the sake of her marriage.

✝

Everything was so chaotic. They landed in Warsaw, Poland, on March 23, 1981, on Bobby's eighth birthday. Maureen's wheelchair was missing. Also, all their luggage would not arrive until three days later. That delayed the trip down to Krakow for three days. When they finally got to Faustina's former convent, Maureen was exhausted. From the beginning, the idea of this whole trip seemed extreme, fanatical, idiotic.

But she tried to be a good sport, and it paid off. Once at the convent, Maureen made her first good confession since she was very young. Afterwards, she felt a closeness to the Lord. She felt herself letting Him in a *little* bit. She was still brash, still mad at God — mad as can be.

One evening, at Faustina's tomb, the group — the Digans, Fr. Seraphim, and a friend of Fr. Seraphim's named Victor D'Agostino — was praying the ninth day of a novena of prayers in which they asked for healing.

"It was about nine o'clock at night," recalls Maureen. "Father Seraphim suggested we pray the Chaplet of the Divine Mercy for a healing. I thought, 'Ah, healing — whatever. This is something you read about in the Bible. It doesn't *really* happen. But I'll go in and go through it just to make them happy.'" Then, inwardly, she heard Sr. Faustina say, "If you ask for my help, I will give it to you."

Maureen responded, "Okay, Faustina, you dragged me to this country so far from home, if you are going to do something, do it now!"

That's when it all happened.

All the pain seemed to drain out of her body. Her swollen leg, which was due to be amputated shortly, went back to its normal size.

"I knew if I looked, every one else would look, so I didn't look," Maureen says.

Bobby, too, had a sudden change. Confined to a wheelchair, he suddenly showed a lot of energy.

"It was unusual how he had a very gleeful smile on his face," Fr. Seraphim later recalled. "We noticed that something was happening with him. He was sort of listless before that." In addition, Fr. Seraphim noticed that Maureen suddenly seemed radiant, peaceful, and calm. Following the prayer, Fr. Seraphim picked Bobby up out of the wheelchair, so that he could place a bouquet of flowers on Sr. Faustina's tomb.

Back at the room, Maureen inspected her leg. The swelling was gone. At first fearful, she didn't say a word to anyone. She slept till 5 o'clock the next afternoon. So did Bobby. As Maureen roused awake, she noticed Bobby sitting up and coloring. This was not ordinary. Sitting up on his own was not something Bobby had been able to do. Then, Maureen looked at her leg. The swelling was still gone. She called her husband over to see.

"Yeah," said Bob. "That's what we came here for. You've been healed."

It took several days for Maureen to accept that she had received a gift of healing from God.

When she returned to the United States, five doctors independently examined her. They each concluded she had been completely healed. They had no medical explanation. The Sacred Congregation for the Causes of Saints, in consultation with a team doctors, examined the accumulated evidence. Then, a team of theologians did the same, followed by a team of cardinals and bishops. The cure was accepted as a miracle brought about through Sr. Faustina's intercession to the Divine Mercy, which led to Faustina's beatification at St. Peter's Square on April 18, 1993.

The Digans say Bobby received a dramatic but incomplete healing. Even during the trip itself, they took him off his seizure medication, something that doctors strongly warn against without medical advice or supervision.

"He didn't even have a twitch," Bob says.

He lived another 10 years. During that time, he learned to ride a bicycle. He played wheelchair basketball. He won gold and silver medals in the Special Olympics. The Digans were planning to buy a special van so that Maureen and Bobby could run errands together and be more independent. By this time, Bob and Maureen had left the city and moved out to western Massachusetts, where they took jobs with the Marians in Stockbridge to help spread the message of Divine Mercy. Believing that Faustina's Divine Mercy revelations contain the prophetic message for our age, Bob left a steady job that provided financial security for a reduction of pay, benefits, and retirement pension.

✝

Life was good for the Digans — stable, *normal*. But in 1989, when Bobby underwent what was expected to be a routine operation to correct scoliosis, an abnormal curving of the spine, it didn't go well. As a result of surgical complications, he became paralyzed and would no longer be able to eat or drink on his own or to walk ever again. His condition suddenly and increasingly deteriorated.

By May 1991, bed-bound, Bobby called his mother into his room. "Mommy," he said, "I have something to tell you. God is going to send His Son, Jesus, to take me to heaven soon. Don't be sad and cry."

He then asked her to send his daddy in.

"I called Bob," recalls Maureen, "and then I went into the bathroom and turned on all the faucets, so Bobby wouldn't hear me crying."

To this day, she and Bob cannot talk about Bobby without it bringing tears. They still miss him terribly.

Bobby, despite his developmental disabilities, prepared for his own death. Though he had little understanding for the arrangement of dates and time, to everyone's amazement, he said he wouldn't be there for his mother's birthday in June, but he'd be there for Mother's Day. He arranged to have one of his nurses fill a planter outside the Digan home with flowers for Mother's Day. He then arranged to have the nurse get his mother flowers for her birthday — flowers, he insisted, "that will never die."

Father Seraphim, who had grown close to Bobby over the years, said the boy had "a fine sense of the spiritual, which was unusual for someone of his age." He recalls how Bobby liked things to be blessed by a priest, so that they had some connection with God. Bobby would recite one very simple, very profound prayer that his parents taught him: "*Mary, I give my heart to you.*"

Father Seraphim was with Bobby during the boy's last moments of life. He recalls how Bobby was unresponsive. They celebrated Holy Mass at his bedside.

"We knew he was going," recalls Fr. Seraphim. "When we came to the moment of Holy Communion, I said, 'Bobby, we are ready to give you Holy Communion. Would you please open your mouth, so we can put some Precious Blood in.'" Bobby opened his mouth very quickly. Father Seraphim dripped some Precious Blood onto Bobby's tongue. Feeling that it was too small of an amount, Fr. Seraphim asked Bobby to open his mouth again.

Bobby "very slowly, and deliberately, opened his mouth. His tongue was cupped. He held it there long enough for me to put a spoonful into it," Fr. Seraphim said. "Slowly, he withdrew his tongue, and slowly, he closed his mouth. It was the most beautiful reception of the Eucharist I had ever seen."

Shortly afterward, Fr. Seraphim, Bob, and Maureen all had their hands on Bobby. On May 23, 1991, at the age of 18, Bobby took his last breath.

Something was certainly afoot. Upon Bobby's death, his whole complexion changed. He no longer looked emaciated. Lying there, he suddenly looked like a healthy boy again. His color returned. His freckles, too. One could even detect a smile on his face.

Four flowers that will never die still hang on Maureen's bedroom wall.

✝

There are other things on other walls: an image of the Divine Mercy, a photo of Bobby on his bicycle, a print of the Last Supper, Maureen and Bob on their wedding day. All these things somehow interrelate. Bob and Maureen sorted it out years ago.

They've sorted out why they think God chose "stubborn Maureen" for a healing.

"It's to prove to people that God does love all of us," Maureen says. "It's us who turn our backs to God. He never turns His back on us, no matter how low we get."

They've sorted out why a miracle happened in this moment of history.

"In our day and age, when everything is so chaotic, and everything seems so discouraging, and there's all this violence, the answer is still very clear: God is still with us," says Bob. "He allowed the healing to take place to let us know that He is still with us. But it is also a preparation for His final coming. We do believe this message of Divine Mercy is the prophetic message for our age, a call for people to turn back to God. Christ told St. Faustina that before He returns as a just Judge, 'I first open wide the door of My mercy. He who refuses to pass through the door of My mercy must pass through the door of My justice'" (*Diary*, 1146).

"We believed God had touched our lives, not for ourselves, but for a witness to the Church," says Bob.

They've sorted out why they think Bobby didn't receive a "complete" healing.

"Bobby's vocation in life was finished," Maureen says. "It was time for him to go home. This is a witness for others that the greatest healing comes in going to the Promised Land."

"Maureen said that Bobby was the one who received the ultimate healing," says Bob.

Bob and Maureen are both retired. As of recently, Maureen contends with diabetes. They're in need of a new minivan that's better equipped for wheelchair access. Comparatively speaking, she's healthy. Bob was ordained to the permanent diaconate in 2011. They've given talks to various groups and conferences from coast to coast and in other countries. Sometimes, it can get weird. Particularly when some misguided souls seem intent on putting too much emphasis on Maureen's healing rather than the message of God's merciful love. Apparently, believing Bob and Maureen hold special sway with the heavens, some people seek to touch them as if magic powder will rub off. And, of course, it doesn't. They receive requests for special prayers as though they have "a special phone line to God."

"We don't," says Bob. "We are just ordinary people living out our faith in a world needing faith. But it's touching and humbling for us that people ask us to pray for them." And they do pray for them. They keep an offering cup in their living room that's set before a large image of Divine Mercy and a relic of St. Faustina. The cup contains all the names of people who request prayers.

"People — even priests — think that because you received a healing you are able to walk on water almost," Maureen says. "You're not. You're no different. I mean, you're different because you have God in your life, but I'm still Maureen. I still fall. I still need confession. I still need God's help and Faustina's help."

Who doesn't?

"Life goes on," Bob says.

Yes, it does. Yet when the earth shakes, Bob and Maureen don't flinch.

They've experienced things far more powerful.

Contact information:
Deacon Bob and Maureen Digan
P.O. Box 537
Lee, MA 01238
e-mail: dmspeakers@gmail.com

Felix Carroll

CHAPTER 2

Wayne Smith

Not by sight, But by faith

What Scripture tells us, and what the Diary of St Faustina tells us, is that God sent His only Son not to condemn us but to save us.

— Wayne Smith

His retinas take in nothing more than a little light set against shadow. His blind man's cane *click-click-clicks* out ahead of him, probing for clear passage on unfamiliar terrain, out onto the rocks at water's edge at Belmont Harbor, where he has come to kill himself.

How will he do it? He'll take one last breath, exhale, and simply jump off the rocks and go under. He'll sink to the bottom, open his mouth, fill his airways with water, and let his bodily reflexes foolishly fight for his survival. That's the plan, anyway.

Cough. Yes, he'll cough underwater. He'll have to. His body will attempt to get that water back out where it belongs, back into that huge lake whose luminescent green-blues he could make out up until the age of eight, when he last could see color, back before his sense of humor grew scornful, back when he first sensed life would not be easy.

Breathe in. The body will fight to survive. The mind will fight to die. He's always been hardheaded. The mind will win this one, he'll tell himself. But first he'll have to yield to this one final offense — having to breathe when he no longer wants to breathe. His body will want to draw in air; it will discover only water. It'll be of no use.

Will it hurt? He doesn't know. Maybe he'll go unconscious before it does. Maybe he'll go into cardiac arrest. The *Chicago Tribune* will probably publish a small item on it, right? About how the body of a 40-year-old blind man was fished out from Lake Michigan. The newspaper blurb will be cut to fit, depending on who was murdered that day or which politician was charged with graft. Maybe the discovery of his body will garner 150 words? Maybe 200? What's the suicide of a blind man worth in editorial space?

The tip of his cane finally slaps against water. *It's snowing, isn't it? Yes, it is.* He turns back around and can make out the broad-shouldered skyline of Chicago. *It really is magnificent, isn't it? All those vertical lines from here to the heavens, plumb against the gush of light from a November sky.* Somewhere in that maze of streets — all that steel and pavement, all those doorways, all those voices, all those shadows he mistakes for solid objects, and all those solid objects he mistakes for shadows

— is the wife he no longer loves. And a five-year-old son he loves, but not enough to overcome his self-pity and despair. And fools who believe in God.

When he hesitates, he hears a voice: "Don't think about it, just do it!" the voice says.

He sets down his cane, takes in a deep breath like he's smelling a bouquet of roses, and then he exhales as if he's blowing out his birthday candles.

Goodbye, Chicago.

He jumps. He disappears under the surface.

✝

Directly behind the ark that holds the Torah scrolls in the reformed Jewish temple of his youth, Wayne Smith one day discovered a small closet, and inside that small closet was a soft drink machine. He was the temple gopher, an energetic boy who sought to please. From then on, while worshippers assembled each week presumably in reverence to the Torah and the Word of God, he was thinking about a Coca-Cola. Behind all the solemnity and ritual of the Sabbath — literally behind all those written laws of the Torah, all those dizzying lists of faceless names and foreign tribes, all those covenants and reckonings, comings and goings, sin and death, punishment and wrath — there was something sweet and simple: a soft drink. All the wonders of the Lord, whatever they might be, couldn't stand a chance.

Long before he convinced himself there was no reason to be on this earth, Wayne Smith had convinced himself there was no reason to believe in God. It was 1959, to be precise. He was 14 years old. The facts were stacked in his favor. These people, neighbors and friends, gathered at the temple each week, but why? Out of faith? Because of tradition? Or worst of all, for appearances only? Whatever the case, his mother would lead him and his younger brother, Gary, to temple each week. He learned Scripture. A bit, anyway, and he wasn't encouraged to ask too many questions. He and Gary giggled when their mother would lay an elbow into the ribcage of their snoring father. That was all fine. But then it wasn't all fine.

Any kid who's curious about life and how to live it eventually asks the big questions, the obvious questions. And if you're a sensitive kid who discovers a soft drink machine behind the Torah, it stands to reason you'll begin to chaff at taking large matters at face value.

Maybe as his sight progressively worsened, his hearing became acute. He tuned in when the rabbi gave a particularly searing sermon, like the one concerning the sin of gossip. The Hebrews have their own lexicon for the degrees of damage inflicted by the evil tongue. *Lashon Hara*: any derogatory or damaging statement. *Rechilut*: any communication that generates animosity between people. Look what happened to the prophetess Miriam in the Book of Exodus when she spoke ill against Moses because of his choice for a wife. God punished her with leprosy. It's right there in Scripture, Wayne would think to himself. Could it be any clearer?

So what happened after this fiery sermon? Wayne was out in the lobby of the temple, and what does he hear? It seemed like in almost every conversation — gossip, whispers, the wagging of tongues.

Religion? This is where the hope of humanity resides? *Really?*

There's a good life to be had for those who follow God's commandments and eagerly await Him? *Really?*

"This is garbage," Wayne thought to himself. "There's no God. People come here because it's a tradition or because it's socially obligatory. It means nothing to them. There's no presence of God here."

✝

He's fully clothed. The water bears down upon his body. He's sinking. The water temperature has to be somewhere in the low 40s, right? But he's not cold. Amazing, isn't it? Not cold at all!

✝

The year he blows out 14 candles, he wishes for a medical breakthrough. Fourteen years old and he's already figured everything out. He's sharp, proud of his bold conclusions, a raw recruit to the bottomlands of atheism.

Fourteen years old, and his world is about to be rocked. Neither his father nor his mother accompanied him on his eye appointment. Wayne wasn't surprised that his father declined to take him. The two were not close. Wayne felt he never measured up to his father's expectations. Rarely could Wayne even catch a baseball. But his mother? Marital problems seemed to have rearranged her priorities. Wayne took the bus downtown by himself. After a quick exam, his ophthalmologist didn't pussyfoot around.

"What do you know about your disease?"

Not much, was the answer. He knew his grandfather had the same disease, but still his grandfather elected to marry and have children. His grandfather was an attorney. He had friends. He lived a full life.

Called *retinitis pigmentosa*, the disease — a congenital deterioration of the retina — is hereditary. Armed with new genetic information — not all of it accurate — the doctor informed Wayne that because his condition is hereditary, if he were to have male children, they'd have the disease. If he had female children, they'd be carriers of the disease. Oh, and within 20 years, Wayne will see nothing but shadows and light, and even those he'll see only barely.

When Wayne walked out of the doctor's office onto Michigan Avenue, he felt like he had just been given a death sentence. He was going to be blind. Lights out.

He had forsaken Judaism, and there was no God. He was alone on Michigan Avenue, and his future literally was going to be very dark.

✝

"Woe unto me."
Didn't Job say that?
"Woe is me now."
Didn't some woman in Leviticus say that?
What's her name?

✝

In school, his affliction increasingly stood out. He wore thick glasses — bottle-glass thick. He could only see through the very center of his lenses, so his head had this natural movement, bobbing and weaving, in an effort for his eyes to piece together a fuller picture of the world before him. Some of the kids took sadistic pleasure in imitating his involuntary head movements. Sometimes, they'd be met with a punch. Wayne had a handicap, true. But he also had a temper and zero tolerance for jerks. So, he spent plenty of time sitting on the radiator in the principal's office. He was a battler.

✝

Water isn't gushing into his lungs as he expected. He rises to the surface and treads the choppy water. He's not chickening out. Not at all. He's determined for the waters to take him. It's Lake Michigan, after all. Ships have gone under here. Lots of them: steamers, schooners, car ferries, yachts.

People drown in these waters every year. Even in the calm waters of summertime. Therefore, drowning on purpose should be a cinch, shouldn't it?

He exhales deeply and disappears till there's nothing but the choppy waves of Lake Michigan, notoriously reluctant to give up its dead.

✝

When you're young and convinced there's no God, what do you do then? Crawl into the fetal position and wait till this nightmare is over with? Run rabid through the streets shouting that the end can't come quickly enough? Sit around in reading circles and congratulate yourself that you read the work of a high-brow existentialist like Jean-Paul Sartre? What do you do?

A self-proclaimed free thinker, Wayne Smith — a physical person, headstrong, predisposed to bear forth wherever it may lead — spent the better part of his adolescence feeling awful. It was time to feel good. The 1960s and 1970s were accommodating. We know how this goes.

Promiscuous sex: *Check.* Whenever the opportunity presented itself. Even with married women. This was encouraged. The nuclear family had proven itself dysfunctional, hadn't it? Let's just wipe out the commitment part of the relationship equation and feel good. Wayne, with his new contact lenses, could still see well enough to set his sights upon the female figures cutting their way through the halls of the urban, high-rise college campus he attended. He was handsome and interesting and iconoclastic.

Drugs: *Check.* He "experimented." What would LSD do to him? Marijuana? Hashish? He didn't know, so why not find out?

Subversive art? *Check.* Among his radical pieces was a line drawing of a woman kneeling and praying. The woman was pregnant. Her distended stomach was comprised of a picture of Sirhan Sirhan cut into the shape of a fetus. Sirhan Sirhan had recently assassinated Bobby Kennedy. The image was anchored with the words, "If you have him, will you still want him?"

Legalized abortion? *Check.* Wayne, dragging the tough years of adolescence behind him — a terrible self-image — figured it better to die than to be born unwanted.

He studied philosophy and discovered the endless ways to look at the world. One person's truth was different from someone else's. There was no *absolute truth.* If you want to be an existentialist, be an existentialist. He figured: your choice. But he drew the line at belief in God. If he heard someone speak of the Bible, he'd say, "Yeah, great. I love good fiction." In so many words, he once told a cloistered monk to get a life.

Still, he always had it in his heart to help people, particularly those who, like him, were treated as outcasts. He detested dogma, but he loved people. He still wished to care for the neediest, those suffering under racism, or the homeless. He believed in the power of good.

But how can there be a God? Look at all the injustice in the world. Look at all the pain and horror. The Holocaust? The Bataan Death March? Children starving in Biafra? What, 55 million people died in World War II? Where was God in all that? He saw the footage of lawmen down South beating blacks. He learned of the Tuskegee experiment. That was right out of the Nazi playbook, wasn't it? He viewed the grainy footage of terrified children in Vietnam running out from under clouds of American-made Napalm, with their skin slipping off their bodies. The camera is on the move, in retreat, jerking all over the place, trying to take it all in, bit by bit.

Sounds familiar.

What are you going to do about it? Take a hit off a joint? Sure.

Tune in?

Turn on?

Drop out?

And by the way, there's a soda machine behind the Torah. How funny is that?

Funny, all right. Hilarious.

✝

Submerged in the waters of Lake Michigan a second time, Wayne opens his mouth for the water to come gushing in, but the water wouldn't even come into his mouth, much less his lungs. It wouldn't cooperate. He was getting angry.

✝

The Associated Press in 1980 wrote a feature story that was picked up in newspapers around the country of a legally blind photographer making a name for himself in Chicago. That was Wayne Smith. They took a photo of him shooting a nature scene and explained how this legally blind man would judge his focusing distance with measuring tape and a magnifying glass.

His parents had bought Wayne a box camera when he was 11 years old. Photography had become a passion. He'd have the film developed and prints made, and he'd hold the images right up to the center of his thick glasses. With photography, he could make the world freeze. It was like a miracle. He immersed himself in a transitory world of vision. Imagine that. He could take his time and study a world at standstill.

He wore contact lenses. By means of the newly instituted Log-MAR eye chart — the now familiar inverted triangle whose letter sizes decrease in a logarithmic progression — Wayne had a corrected 20/200 vision and a field of vision of less than five degrees. His eyesight was progressively getting worse. He was determined to see what he could see while he still could see. With his camera, he had a talent for capturing tension in street life. Making sorties out into nature, he'd come across scenes that looked God-sent, but "there was no God," so maybe it was blind luck. Iridescent fog appearing and disappearing. The light and shadows of trees and water. Beautiful. Surreal. He became enraptured with seeing.

This being in the years before 1991 when the Americans with Disabilities Act was signed into law, few companies would hire a legally blind man. He eventually found work in — of all places — an employment agency, as an employment counselor. His photography — taking portraits and nature scenes — became a side career.

By 1980, he was married. Despite the hereditary medical risks outlined by his doctor years prior, he "caved in" to his wife's desire for a child. Along came a boy in 1985, all nine pounds of him. They named him Ryan. When Wayne first held him, he was smitten. He changed diapers and burped him in the middle of the night. If Ryan threw up or had diarrhea, Wayne cleaned it up, finding the offending fluid by touch. Making sacrifices for him quickly became a joy. This is the point at which the angry atheist finds peace and gets his life together and lives happily ever after, right? No, not at all. Wayne loved his wife, but they fought a lot. He loved his son, but not enough to put him first on his priority list.

He loved seeing, and maybe that's what he loved most of all. But the visual world was fading from view, even with his corrective lenses. By 1990, his photography had become hackneyed — cockeyed, out of focus, containing things that weren't supposed to be in there. Because he had a deep respect for photography, he pulled the plug on his photography career. He put out ads, and people came by one by one, handed him cash, and took away his equipment until everything was gone.

"There's no God. There's no meaning. There's no such thing as love. There's nothing here in this world for me anymore," Wayne concluded. In his misery, in his selfishness, in his delirium, he put on his coat, didn't say goodbye to his wife and child, shut the apartment door behind him, stepped out into the snow and *click, click, clicked* his way to his own death.

✝

Maybe Wayne just can't do anything right, including drown himself. He goes under five times, and the water will not enter his airways. It's as if a hand is covering his mouth. He wants it over with, but he won't get off that easy.

Angry, confused, he heads back to shore where he hears a man's voice say, "Take my hand." Wayne reaches up and takes the hand, but the hand feels so small and frail, and Wayne is fearful that instead of being helped out of the water, he'll accidentally pull the man in.

Wait, isn't that a good sign? In the midst of despair, he realizes he's concerned about someone else? That's a good sign, right?

Wayne is back up on the rocks. The man hands Wayne his cane, which he is unable to find by himself. Who is this man who appears and offers help out of nowhere? Wayne has no clue and no opportunity to inquire. The skies have grown darker. The man helps him get back up to the road and gives Wayne $25 to get a cab.

He's still sopping wet when he steps back inside his home.

"Daddy, why are you all wet?" Ryan asks.

"I tried to die, and I failed," Wayne responds.

Twenty-one years later, Wayne is in his apartment off Lakeshore Drive preparing for his bi-monthly radio show on Radio Maria.

"That's how far gone I was," Wayne says. "Pretty disgusting. I was supposed to be dead, and I wasn't, and I didn't love Ryan enough to do anything about it. I didn't love my wife and myself either. It was despair, total despair."

That day at the harbor, and that fragile hand that reached for him, didn't turn out to be his St. Paul moment. God didn't knock Wayne off his proverbial horse and make him see the light. Wayne proceeded to drink too much. He felt as though he were under demonic attack. He desired women other than his wife. He eventually sought psychological help, but then proceeded to become infatuated with his counselor. The counselor gave him terrible, immoral advice regarding marriage and sex. A long stream of failures and conflicts in his marriage finally brought his wife to the end of her rope, and she divorced him. Wayne would keep a close relationship with his son Ryan.

Suddenly single, Wayne was on the front steps to his apartment building one day when a stranger walked by and said to him out of the blue, "When I'm in trouble, I ask God for help."

Just like that. A younger Wayne Smith would have made a wisecrack. The older Wayne Smith was tired of wisecracks. He got up, caught a bus, and went into Temple Sholum on Lakeshore Drive where he sat alone not knowing what to do. He had never, of his own accord, gone to a house of God to pray. He didn't believe in God, let alone a God who could hear him and who loved him. Yet, still he sat there and said, "God, I don't even know if You're there. If You exist, there's no reason why You should help me because I've done a lot of terrible things. But I have no place else to go, so I'm asking for Your help."

That was his first prayer since the age of 14 and probably the first prayer he had ever prayed with sincerity.

He waited for something to happen, some kind of acknowledgment that God heard him — a beam of light, a warm glow, a thunder-throated Don LaFontaine-like voice saying, "Yes, Wayne, I've heard you."

Nothing. Silence, but for the sound of traffic outside.

"I'm on my own. Either there is no God, or He will not help me because of the things I have done," Wayne concluded.

He stayed awhile and cried a lot. Then, he grabbed his cane.

But within seconds of walking out onto the street, he was filled with the most incredible joy he had ever known. He went from total despair to ecstasy.

✝

Just like that: He was given the gift of faith.

That voice out on the rocks that told him to jump — that was the Devil seeking to collect a soul. That became clear to him. The hand of God blocked his mouth to prevent him from drowning. That became clear, too. That man on the rocks who held out his frail hand was some merciful angel seeking to end the misery of another. That monk he once offended had probably went on to pray for him.

Just like that: God exists.

But as he thought about it, Wayne knew he wasn't supposed to go back to temple. He put two and two together and concluded that because he didn't receive the gift of faith *in* the temple, but *outside*, he was to search for a spiritual home in a different denomination. He was to find the path by which to encounter God and to learn, after all these years, who He really was.

Wayne shopped around.

The Jehovah's Witnesses told him that only their denomination would be saved on Doomsday. That sounded absurd, so Wayne politely showed them the door.

In a private appointment with a Buddhist priest, Wayne told him everything that was going wrong in his life: blindness, a broken marriage, no desire to live, no career, no future. The priest interrupted him, came around the desk, grabbed Wayne by the shoulders, pulled him out of the chair, and said, "Thank your hands. Thank your feet. Thank your heart. Thank your lungs, and get out of here." The point was well taken: Be grateful for what you do have. That helped. Greatly, in fact. Still, Buddhism wasn't for him.

Puzzled as to where to go from there, Wayne went down to the lagoon in Lincoln Park near Stockton Drive. He sat on a bench and marveled at what he saw: the reflections of trees on the water, and then the sun coming in and out of the clouds.

"God was giving me a gift," Wayne says today. "Just so beautiful. He calmed me down and brought me to something beautiful."

While walking home, he passed St. Michael's Catholic Church in Old Town. Well-dressed people were rushing in. Wayne felt compelled to enter, too, but decided to come back when so much activity had subsided, and that's what he did. The church was empty and dark. He felt around with his cane for a place to sit, settling in a pew beside a pillar. He recalls feeling at home and at peace.

"I wanted to be there," he says, "to think about things and also to not think." Because his son's elementary school was nearby, he began a routine of spending some time at St. Michael's before meeting Ryan.

"I started to realize God wants me there," Wayne recalls. "I started talking to God. I didn't know about the tabernacle, so I didn't know He was there looking right at me, loving me."

One day in St. Michael's, an image came to his mind of Jesus crucified. He prayed to God for the privilege of *really* seeing Him on the cross, so he felt his way up the center aisle toward the altar, walking till he couldn't walk any further. He couldn't see anything, but he had gone looking for Jesus crucified, and to him that meant one thing and one thing only:

He was going to be a Catholic.

He went through the Rite of Christian Initiation for Adults at St. Michael's, a Redemptorist parish that has the mission to promote devotion to Our Lady of Perpetual Help. He got involved in a prayer group. For the first time, he prayed the Chaplet of the Divine Mercy and learned through the message of Divine Mercy and the Gospels that God's greatest attribute was mercy: not anger, not finger-pointing, not judgment.

"Growing up, I was taught about the Old Testament God, a God who could slay a man or a whole people," Wayne says. "Sin displeases Him, and sinners could be dead in an instant. He wasn't presented to me as a warm, loving, affectionate God. I've since learned the Scriptures are filled with His mercy. But I was left with this wrong idea."

Eventually, Wayne would spend the better part of the next nine years working for low wages at a Franciscan ministry that provides food and shelter for the poor and homeless. He realized at the time that 35 years of being an atheist led to his suicide attempt, but nine years of serving the poor brought him more fulfillment than he had ever experienced.

Still, all was not well. He was lustful. His sexual sins kept him from union with God, he says. He served two masters. "And I was miserable and tormented," he recalls. "I had invited the Devil into my life many years ago. Satan knows our weaknesses. I wanted to give my full life, everything, to God and serve Him through serving His people, but my sinfulness was distracting me."

Spiritually sidetracked, he spoke with some close friends about his efforts to live a celibate, single life. They asked him, "Why are you doing this to yourself? Did you ask God if celibacy is what He wants for you?"

"They were right," says Wayne.

Before the Blessed Sacrament one day, he finally prayed, "Lord, I need to love and be loved. I need to touch and be touched."

God sent him Miriam.

✝

The red light is on. They're live on air. Headphones on, microphones in front of them, Miriam and Wayne are face to face across a wide table in the second-story studios of Radio Maria, which overlook St. Stanislaus Koska, the official Divine Mercy sanctuary in the Archdiocese of Chicago.

"*Today's program,*" Miriam tells listeners in Spanish, "*is titled 'God loves You.'*"

"*What better way to explain God's love than through His Divine Mercy,*" Wayne says in English.

The two first met at a café just around the corner from these studios. Each had attended a Holy Mass and prayer service on the feast of the Annunciation at St. Stanislaus one evening. They dated. They fell in love. In Wayne, Miriam saw a life partner who bears powerful witness to the truth of merciful love.

"This is what the world needs to know about — about God's love for us and what can happen when we turn in trust to God. Wayne is proof of that promise," says Miriam, a cradle Catholic and native of Toluca, outside Mexico City.

Wayne knew that Miriam coming into his life was nothing short of a miracle. In addition to praying for the love of a woman, Wayne had been praying separately for a ministry partner — but not just *any* ministry partner. He gave God a wish list. He wanted a partner who spoke Spanish and English. He prayed that his ministry partner would be a woman in particular who had a "mother's heart" and who sought to serve others, particularly those in great spiritual distress.

In Miriam, God sent both a romantic love *and* a ministry partner. Together, they run their ministry, Not By Sight Media, which makes use of his conversion story as well as focuses on the importance of family, the sanctity of life, and how faith can guide people through every kind of trial and crisis.

"Being Catholic is not for spectators," Wayne says.

✝

The doctor was right. Wayne is almost completely blind now. He says he sees now "through the love of God and through the kind heart and eyes of Miriam."

"She's taught me what unconditional love is," Wayne says. "I didn't know what love was and didn't understand how much God loves me until I saw her love and God loving through her."

For his part, Wayne taught her to rediscover the treasure of the Catholic faith, and how to "serve God the way God deserves," Miriam says.

Wayne proposed to Miriam on Pentecost Sunday in 2011. They were married at St. Stanislaus Koska on Oct. 7, 2011, the feast of the Holy Rosary. On their wedding day, Wayne asked the Lord for the gift of sight for just a moment, so he could see Miriam's face.

"I could see her glowing there," he says. "Her dress was beautiful and white. The church was filled with sunlight. I tried to see her when she was coming down the aisle, and I couldn't. But when she came up beside me, I took her hand, and I asked the Lord to allow me to see her. I could see her radiance. She's very easy to see."

For their honeymoon, they traveled by train to the National Shrine of The Divine Mercy in Stockbridge, Massachusetts. "We wanted to be there to thank God for His mercy in bringing us together," says Wayne.

✝

"Jesus Christ came to this earth for one reason," Wayne tells his listeners. *"He came in response to the love of the Father for a fallen people. What Scripture tells us, and what* the Diary of St. Faustina *tells us, is that God sent His only Son not to condemn us but to save us."*

On the radio show, Wayne doesn't lecture as if from on a mountaintop. He's down to earth. He speaks with humility. He knows conversion is an ongoing experience. On the radio show, he speaks in English of the mercy of God, and Miriam speaks in Spanish of *divina misericordia*. It's the same language — the language of healing through God.

After the show, he and Miriam thank the woman who runs the soundboard. They say so long to the station manager. They bundle up in their coats, and they sling their bags over their shoulders.

Together, Wayne and Miriam take the small elevator down to ground level and step out into a chilly evening. Arm and arm, they *click, click, click* their way down into the subway, back up onto the street, through the crowds, and through all those lights and all those shadows.

They *click, click, click* through this city where a man can get lost if not for love.

Courtesy of Reeves County Detention Center

CHAPTER 3

Silvano Toso

Finally Free

Jesus to St. Faustina:

Your great trust in Me forces Me to continuously grant you graces. You have great and incomprehensible rights over My Heart, for you are a daughter of complete trust.

— Diary of St. Faustina, 718

Tumbleweeds dash like fugitives across the flat, barren, drought-scorched land. A stop sign is shot full of holes. Letters on the town's welcome sign have either twisted in a pounding west Texas wind or have flaked off entirely. Just beyond the welcome sign and behind the gnarl of desert brush, a yellow billboard — half collapsed — is intended to say, "Remember to Keep Holy the Sabbath."

For those inclined to see the symbolism, this billboard could mean one of two things: Its message has proven futile, or the messenger has moved on. The latter seems more likely. Pecos, Texas, seems in the process of being reclaimed by the desert dust. Many of its downtown roofs are sagging. Most of its businesses are shuttered. Its downtown streets are nearly deserted. A ghostly set of bleachers lines West Second Street, presumably set up for a parade that came and went and probably won't come back.

In the hard-bitten outskirts, a man outside a Walmart has set up a table and sells crucifixes made from barbed wire. A couple of new hotels cater to truckers along the sparsely traveled Interstate-20. Under a blaring sun, a cowboy rides a dirt road on horseback. Beyond him are the silhouettes of pump jacks rocking like stationary carousel horses. And beyond them are a group of low-slung buildings wrapped in a glittering assemblage of razor wire. This is Pecos' largest employer: Reeves County Detention Center, a federal prison housing 3,760 inmates. Among those is a man born 6,000 miles away in Italy, who needs no reminding of the Sabbath Day and whose heart was once as tumbledown as his current surroundings. For him, Pecos might as well be a world away, but this prison and this town serve as a perfect backdrop for a story of how God can cultivate life from barrenness.

✝

A steel door opens in the visiting room of Reeves County Detention Center, and in steps inmate number 77806-004, led by a guard. The thick door closes with a clunk, and the inmate — dressed in prison-issued gray shirt and pants — takes a seat at a round, steel table bolted to the floor. His name is Silvano Toso.

Born near Venice, as a boy, he dreamed of being a priest, dreamed of learning everything there was to know, and dreamed of making his mark in the world. He never became a priest. But he can speak knowledgeably about things like architecture, music, economics, history, and botany — even tumbleweeds. In matters of business, he made his mark. Then, everything went wrong.

"I lost everything: my wife, my money, my good name," he says. "Everything. I lost it all."

He looks a little like the film star Robert De Niro, leaning in on his elbows, able to frown and smile at the same time, and with eyes that squint and twinkle as if identifying silhouettes in shadowy corners and calling them out to account for themselves.

On August 29, 2008, federal agents in south Florida banged on Silvano's door, handcuffed him, and incarcerated him. He declines to get into specifics of the case, only to say that he led a sinful life — not criminal, but sinful — of which he is deeply ashamed. His arrest stemmed from the "possession of illegal documents while he was working on behalf of the Italian government." He pled guilty. His sentence extends into late 2013 when he'll be 62 years old.

He lives in a prison unit shared with 50-plus other inmates. It's an open room. There is no privacy to speak of. Even the toilets and showers have no walls or partitions. He's learned to walk on eggshells. He's learned to abide by the unwritten rules of the inmate power structure. His cot is set against a wall, and he is grateful for that because there's a water valve beside his cot that he can use as a shelf to prop up an image of Jesus, the Divine Mercy, and a photo of his granddaughter. "She was born smiling," he says.

He owns a set of colored pencils with which he draws images of Jesus, St. Faustina, the Blessed Virgin Mary, and the Stations of the Cross, and with which he prepares notices, in both English and Spanish, of prayer services he's arranged for fellow inmates. He keeps a spiritual journal. It serves as a powerful testament to how God works in souls. Of the Blessed Virgin Mary, he writes on April 15, 2011:

... I wish I could live 1,000 years to devote all my tears to console her broken heart. Why am I so wicked and miserable? O my Jesus, please take my misery as a token of love toward You and Your sweet Mother, because I truly do not want to sin anymore.

On March 1, 2009, he writes:

But I remembered what once a confessor told me: "Never doubt if a sin has been forgiven to you in confession. The doubt in itself would be a sin against the Divine Mercy."

He has no doubt God has forgiven him. But doubts are one thing; regrets are another. He's got plenty of those.

When his daughter Bianca was two years old, he used to walk with her hand in hand through the streets at dusk. If they stopped for a rest at an outdoor café, she would make a point of it to visit each table and announce, "He is my Papa." She was so happy, she had to tell the whole world. She's grown up now and lives in Australia, and she's married with a young daughter of her own. Bianca maintains a relationship with her father through handwritten letters. They exchange Christmas cards and birthday wishes. What he wouldn't give to go back in time and hold her hand and walk with her through the streets, a proud papa. What he wouldn't give now to have a do-over.

Raised in an orphanage because his widowed mother hadn't the means to care for him, Silvano would have listened with more attention to Sr. Celina, who oversaw his care. She taught him about God and the angels. She told him he should "live to convert souls," and that he should be "pure, pure, and again pure." As a boy, he imagined himself a missionary priest in Africa, China, and India, a modern-day Marco Polo — a fellow Venetian — bringing to the world's furthest reaches not the riches of gold but the Word of God. He once asked the monks who gave him Holy Communion if the Hosts were made with honey. They weren't. "But it tastes so sweet," he said. Jesus was the brother he never had. Once, when he was 11 years old, a priest found him in an empty chapel knocking on the tabernacle. He was innocently seeing if Jesus was at home and if He had time to spend with him.

What he wouldn't give to go back in time knowing what he knows now.

Would his wife of 27 years have left him? Would he have allowed his business successes in Australia, Italy, and the United States to crush him under the weight of his own hubris? The upper echelon in Italian government had him on speed dial. He was an upstanding man. Just look at him, dressed in the plumage of the Knights of Columbus.

Look at his name in the papers from all his successes on behalf of the dispossessed. He was instrumental in overturning complex government policies and restrictions in order to give grape growers in Australia a fair cut of the grapes' trade profits. He was instrumental in securing pensions for Italian nationals living in Florida. He was a businessman to be reckoned with.

And a holy one to boot, right? He hobnobbed with priests and bishops. He opened his checkbook and made things happen. Toward his latter years, he fooled them all. He fooled himself. At the conclusion of Sunday Mass, he would genuflect before the Lord, then turn on his heels and resume a wretched life of "adult entertainment" and pride.

He now reckons that when the Feds came knocking, it was probably the best thing that could have ever happened to him, under the circumstances. But, good gracious, what he wouldn't give to have a do-over.

✝

The prison visiting area — of polished white tile, concrete walls, and a bank of vending machines — has the sterile, characterless feel of a hospital cafeteria, though prison officials have tried to make it as welcoming as possible. On one concrete wall, there are paintings of Disney and Looney Tune characters, like Goofy and Porky Pig and Sylvester and Tweety Bird, geared to the many children of inmates who visit on weekends. The children now visiting quietly play with blocks, or sit on their fathers' laps, or run around laughing as if there's nothing odd about the circumstances.

The license plates out in the visiting parking lot indicate that families have traveled from as far away as Minnesota, California, Georgia, and Mexico to visit their incarcerated loved ones. Together, families eat sandwiches and drink beverages from the vending machines and play cards or talk quietly.

This is the first visit Silvano has had since he was transferred here from a prison in Florida in 2009. His daughter has never had the means to make the trip. His second wife, an American, maintains correspondence with him, but they have agreed the marriage is, by all intents and purposes, over. So he doesn't expect to ever see her again. He has no idea why he was transferred here to Pecos, of all places, in the summer of 2009, and it would be of no use asking anyone, anyway, because it really doesn't matter. They brought him here in a white van, and when the time comes for his release, they'll drive him out of here in a van, put him on a plane, and send him back to Italy or to Australia — his choice. But he won't be permitted to stay in the United States.

Nearly all the inmates are Mexicans. Silvano is the only Italian. But they share Catholicism — at least most of them do. The inmates call him "Toso Famoso" (Famous Toso), but mostly they don't call him anything at all. Mostly, they leave him alone to his prayers, his reading, and his artwork. They agree to allow him to watch a daily Mass broadcast on channel 28, at 7 a.m. each morning.

On another wall in the visiting room, there's a mural of Pecos. It's an idealized portrait. The land is a luscious green. A tire swing hangs from a sturdy tree branch. A tractor is impeccably maintained. The fields flourish with crops. And birds flitter above. The green gives way to smooth contours of a painted desert. The mural could be a cruel hoax, if you chose to see it that way — if you're a prisoner aching for freedom into the wide expanses.

But Silvano's memories don't fail him. He doesn't romanticize the things of this world. He sees the robins, the bronzed cowbirds, and canyon wrens flying over the razor wire, alighting upon the prison yard's industrial-sized lampposts, and then darting back over to the parking lot and the scrub brush beyond. The paradox of it all no longer fazes him. We all have our own prisons. We all have our own liberties. He knows this now. Spiritually, he has made a clean, concerted break toward holiness.

Indeed, everything changed for him — his heart, his mind, his dreams — on the day an officer made the rounds with a cart full of books from the prison lending library. He had seen a specific book in previous rounds. It had a brown jacket and an image of a nun on the cover, and she looked pretty darn serious. It had caught his eye, but he chose from the other options. But this time, the book seemed to scream at him: "Read me, read me!" He figured why not. He took it. It was called *The Life of Faustina Kowalska: The Authorized Biography*, by an American nun named Sr. Sophia Michalenko, CMGT. He opened it up and was mesmerized as he read about this Polish mystic of the 20th century and her extraordinary visions that gave rise to the Divine Mercy devotions and a Gospel message tailored to the times.

He read of how Christ instructed her to write down words directed to the whole world, of how without cooperating with His grace, we are nothing but sin and wickedness. He read the many things Jesus told her, such as: "Your great trust in Me forces Me to continuously grant you graces. You have great and incomprehensible rights over My Heart, for you are a daughter of complete trust" *(Diary of St. Faustina, 718)*.

He gained from this a newfound knowledge of human "misery" — the knowledge that without God we are nothing and that merit lies in the will.

Silvano couldn't put the biography down. He wrote to Sr. Sophia — who is the sister to world-renowned Divine Mercy scholar Fr. Seraphim Michalenko, MIC, who served as the vice-postulator for Faustina's canonization cause. To Silvano's delight, Sr. Sophia wrote back to him, and, for a time, she became his spiritual guide. Through her book and their correspondence, Silvano learned of the Chaplet of Divine

Mercy, an intercessory prayer given to the world through St. Faustina. Jesus attached extraordinary promises to those who pray the chaplet, including: "Even if there were a sinner most hardened, if he were to recite this Chaplet only once, he would receive grace from My infinite mercy" (*Diary*, 687).

He began praying it every day. He still does. He'll do so for the rest of his life, he says. When prison officials allow, he arranges group prayer with inmates, and they pray the chaplet together. Silvano experienced extraordinary graces almost immediately. He suddenly had peace of mind for the first time since he was a boy innocently knocking on the door of the tabernacle. Prayers were answered.

When a prison official asked for prayers for a medical issue she was having, he prayed to St. Faustina and heard in his heart that the official should go to confession and receive Holy Communion. The prison official did and, later, heartily thanked him. He prayed a Divine Mercy novena for the wife of a deacon who ministers to inmates. The deacon's wife had been diagnosed with cancer. A medical screening soon revealed the cancer was gone. He continually gets assurance that God hears his every prayer.

He prays every day for his fellow inmates. He prays not for his early release. Rather, he prays for the great grace that a prison guard will call his name and lead him to a room with a priest or deacon who will "feed my soul the Body and Blood of Christ," he says. Inmates only sporadically have access to Holy Mass and Holy Communion. Silvano resorts to "spiritual communion" with Christ whereby, through prayer with sincerity, humility, and a desire to follow in Christ's footsteps in acts of faith and charity, he beseeches the Lord's divine assistance.

Time is all he has. He once did the math and figured out that if every one of the 1.25 billion Catholics in the world each prayed 100 chaplets dedicating each to a soul of the Blessed Virgin Mary's choice, they would help God save the souls of all the estimated 109 billion people who have lived on the earth since the days of Noah.

Silvano got hold of a copy of St. Faustina's *Diary* itself in 2009 on the feast of St. Lucy, patron saint of the blind. His daughter sent it to him after he responded to her letter inquiring what he wanted for Christmas. "From there, there was no looking back," he says. "God hooked me up totally and fully and said to me: 'Now you are Mine.'" He read it each day. It took him two years to get through it all because, he says, "each page is a bombshell."

Handwritten bookmarks jut from the pages with notes that show the kinship between him and Faustina: "Yes, I know!" says one such note. And "I did it, too!" says another. Half of its pages are dog-eared. Its cover is threadbare. The book looks as if it were mistakenly put through the wash. But it's worn through sheer love. It was his soul that was put through the wash, his heart that was cleansed.

"She took me to the depths of knowledge," he says. "I learned finally the importance that Jesus gives to each soul. He leaves 99 good souls to search for the missing one. He demanded souls and souls and souls from St. Faustina. There are so many single souls who are missing. Poor Jesus needs some help. So there is a lot to do, and as St. Faustina pointed out, so little time."

He has since filled page after page of his own spiritual journal, this from May 6, 2010:

> *Who cares if I am in prison. Who cares if I am not outside enjoying my life. Who cares if all of my projects, big or small, have come to a halt. I am finally doing what I was supposed to do since I was seven. Help save souls by the bunch.*

Or this from June 21, 2010:

> *To St. Faustina ... You are my guide. Please continue to be my special friend and take me to Jesus and Mary. O Sister Faustina, please take care of me.*

When, in June 2010, he reemerged from a two-week span in which he had felt utterly abandoned by the Lord — a "dark night of the soul," he says — he knelt by his bed, prayed the chaplet, and saw an image in his mind of him holding the bloodied, broken Body of Jesus in his arms. Intensely, for the first time in his life, Silvano comprehended what he had only known in the abstract: that Jesus died for the sins of mankind. He realized, "We are to be love, love," he recalls. "Whenever we do something against love, we go against our own nature, which is also the nature of God." Like Faustina, he has a special relationship with the Lord, whom, he says, speaks to his heart.

"He is a man who wants to do the will of God," says his confessor, Fr. Pedro Garcia, who serves a parish in Michigan, but ministers to inmates in his native Pecos when he comes home to visit. "He works very hard at it. He teaches the other inmates about the faith. He worries that they are not being exposed to the full Church and its teachings. But I see what he's doing. He is a very sincere man, a very good man, and the inmates respect him."

✝

The day he was incarcerated, Silvano weighed 242 pounds. Now, he's a trim and healthy 165 pounds. He's gotten rid of the baggage. When he goes back into society, he plans to travel light as well. He thinks he will probably take up his daughter on her offer to live in Australia, back in the town where he raised her. He envisions working for the poor and keeping a low profile. The powerful businessman will get down to the business of helping the Lord save souls.

"I was an executive my whole adult life," he says. "I know a good deal when I see it."

He'll leave prison knowing things he never knew before: That Satan is real, but that he's an idiot.

"He doesn't stand a chance to those who turn from sin and unite themselves with the Lord," Silvano says.

He knows he was put into prison to be rescued.

He knows that all else is secondary to striving for the love of God.

He knows never to pray "mechanically" — that when he says the "Our Father," God is listening.

The most dramatic change for him is that he no longer views God as an "abstract theological being" but as a real, loving, merciful Person to be loved, and religion is not merely a "code to good conduct and merit" but a Father-to-son relationship, a relationship based on love, trust, and humility. He says that Sr. Sophia Michalenko taught him that.

He knows that life moves moment by moment and that every moment is an opportunity for conversation or a booby-trap to sinfulness.

He longs for two things:

For silence. How wonderful that will be, because he gets none of that here.

Mostly, he longs for the moment when he will step into a church and kneel before the Blessed Sacrament.

"And when I kneel down before Him, I will ask Him how He's doing. He likes to be asked that."

Until then, he is a resident of Pecos, Texas.

✝

"Do you know about tumbleweeds?" Silvano asks. *He* does. As a boy, he would read books on anything and everything, including botany. He felt duty-bound. He would think, "What if an apocalypse came and he were the last man standing?" He figured he would need to know everything so that the rebuilding of civilization could begin. He was too young at the time to factor in that the last man standing would need a last woman standing. Still, at least he took initiative.

"A tumbleweed," he says, "is an amazing thing."

He explains that once it matures, the tumbleweed retracts its roots and yields to the whims and ways of the wind. It looks as though it's nothing but dead, dried twigs, but it's dispersing seeds as it tumbles. And after its come to a dead stop, it absorbs water once again.

"Amazing, isn't it?" says the man who was all but dead, but who tumbled till he came to standstill upon the baptismal waters of the Divine Mercy.

Felix Carroll

CHAPTER 4

Angelina Steenstra

'Though Its Sins Be as Scarlet'

From today on, do not fear God's judgment, for you will not be judged.

— Diary of St. Faustina, 374

Something in her heart told her don't go inside. But she went in, and hours later she was raped. She was only 15 years old.

Today, when she leads rallies and holds a sign that says, "I Regret My Abortion," Angelina Steenstra will recall that night on Easter weekend in 1972. She attended a party thrown by a group of teens she had only recently met. She was desperate to make friends. Inside, the kids were smoking pot and drinking alcohol. Against her better judgment, she joined in. She hadn't eaten, and on an empty stomach, it didn't take long for the alcohol and drugs to go to her head. She lost track of time.

She recalls looking around the room at one point and discovering nearly everyone was gone except for the 17-year-old boy whom she had met at a bonfire a couple weeks prior. He was the one who had invited her to the party. In longing for connection and acceptance, she could imagine becoming someone's girlfriend. In this case with this boy, there would be no courtship, no dates to the movies, no bringing him home to meet the parents, no long, tender phone conversations into the night.

Instead, he took her hand and led her up to a bedroom and sat her down. She recalls pleading with him, "No, no, no, stop!" He didn't stop.

Nearly 12 weeks later, the trauma she experienced by the rape gave way to something far more traumatic for her: an abortion.

✝

What was clear to her co-workers, but not clear to Angelina herself, was that she might be pregnant. Working the morning shift at a diner, Angelina was showing signs of morning sickness when a co-worker recommended she take a pregnancy test. The advice rattled Angelina such that she felt compelled to break the silence of what had happened to her. Her co-worker tried to comfort her. If you're pregnant, "your problem could be easily resolved," she said to Angelina.

A couple weeks passed, and the co-worker followed up to see if Angelina had taken a pregnancy test. Angelina still hadn't.

She was in complete denial. At that point, her co-worker warned her, "There isn't much time if you are going to do something about it," and she directed Angelina to call an abortion clinic advertised in the newspaper.

Now petrified, Angelina took a home pregnancy test, and it revealed she was indeed pregnant. She called the phone number of the abortion facility. From there, it was like a runaway train that couldn't be stopped.

The woman on the other end of the line was skilled in selling abortions to panicked, pregnant teens, and she capitalized on Angelina's fears. Angelina was told that having a baby at 15 years old could ruin her life. Is this what she wanted? No. Her family, her friends, and her community would probably reject her. She would be a single mother and unable to finish high school. Is this what she wanted? No. She was told in no uncertain terms that her entire life hinged upon her making "the right choice."

A lonely teen, Angelina had already felt she didn't belong. Having a child would only clinch the deal, wouldn't it? Is this what she wanted? No. And what about the boy who got her pregnant? Where was he? He wanted nothing more to do with Angelina.

It was settled. She *had* no choice. She made the appointment. On a hot and humid day in July, two acquaintances drove Angelina across the Canadian border into nearby Buffalo, New York, where the clinic was located. They dropped her off, then headed back home to go to work.

Angelina entered the clinic and handed over $250 that she had borrowed from a friend. Then, she signed a waiver that would absolve the clinic should something go wrong during the procedure. There was no counseling provided. The word "baby" was never uttered. Nothing much was said at all other than that the procedure would be quick and wouldn't hurt.

The doctor came in wearing the prototypical white coat. For years afterward, not cognizant of it, every time Angelina would have to go to the doctor, it would trigger fear, sometimes panic. Also, the high-pitched squeal of the vacuum aspirator would come to haunt her. It sounded like a dentist drill. For years afterwards, she would avoid going to the dentist unless it was an emergency, and she would also find herself getting unreasonably angry when vacuuming at home. No clue why. For years, hot and humid days would trigger anxiety. No clue why.

Only when under the bright lights of the operating room, her ankles in stirrups, did Angelina begin to comprehend the magnitude of her decision. When the doctor leaned in to begin the procedure, Angelina wanted to shout, "*Stop!*" But she didn't have the courage. She closed her eyes tightly to the bright lights as the doctor pushed icy instruments into her body. The pain was excruciating. She started crying. They told her to stay still, but she couldn't stop crying. The pain wasn't just physical. She cried in spiritual agony, too. Up till that point, she had never equated "pregnancy" with a "baby."

"Is there a baby in there? Is there a soul?"

Only now had those questions come to her.

When she opened her eyes, she saw a glass jar beside her right foot. With the whirr of the aspirator, the jar filled up with blood.

On the way back over the border, Angelina looked at her reflection in the window of the bus and thought to herself: "You are never going to be able to fix this. You cannot undo this."

Her life then spun out of control.

✝

When Angelina had her abortion in 1972, the attitude was that the procedure — not just the *procedure* but the *decision* itself to have one — was a non-event or simply an unpleasant solution to the more unpleasant problem of an unwanted pregnancy. No one talked about any long-term effects — guilt, anxiety, depression, flashbacks, and suicidal thoughts. You weren't supposed to experience those repercussions, so you talked yourself out of believing you were having them.

Following her abortion, Angelina spent the next seven years self-destructing. Drugs. Alcohol. Serial sexual partners. She woke up most mornings, looked in the mirror, and hated who she saw.

She hated the person she had become. She hated how far she had strayed from the girl she used to be.

That girl she used to be loved building forts with her brothers or helping them carve roads in the sand for their toy cars. She loved to ride her bicycle and to sing in the Glee Club. She loved the outdoors — to go on long car rides in the country and look at cows and hay fields and apples dangling from trees after the first frost. She loved hearing about the saints. She loved in particular the story of Kateri Tekakwitha — since canonized — known as the "Lily of the Mohawks." This Native American and Catholic convert was scarred by smallpox, banished by her tribe, but unshaken in her faith.

The girl she used to be would say her prayers at night. Prayer brought her peace despite the turmoil all around her. While the girl she used to be knew joy and peace, what she didn't know much about was a father's love. The oldest of seven children, she was raised in a family often put on edge under the oppression of an alcoholic father.

Soon after her 15th birthday, Angelina went to live with a neighboring family because things had gotten so bad at home. On the evening that would haunt her for the rest of her life, she lied to her new caretakers. She told them she was going to visit her family. Instead, the girl she used to be went to that party where her innocence was erased.

✝

It would take years to put the pieces together and make sense of it. None of this — not the rape, not the abortion — occurred randomly, she believes. They occurred against a backdrop in which many social mores had been upended, particularly relating to sex. What was once wrong was now right, and what was once right was now wrong. Sex was openly discussed, if not encouraged. By the time Angelina's generation came of age, secularism and immorality had become by all intents and purposes implemented as the social law of the land. She was taught that Church teachings were ancient and impractical.

And when a woman — or a girl — discovered she was pregnant, she was led to believe a fetus was not "an actual human being." Moreover, if you grieved over your abortion, chances were you did so on your own. Indeed, as much as the legalization of abortion was viewed as a milestone in women's liberation, no one really wanted to talk about the actual procedure itself, and certainly few wanted to discuss any negative implications. That's because to do so would undercut the narrative that the legalization of abortion constituted progress in a sophisticated civilization.

At what seemed like the height of her self-destructive period, when she was in university, Angelina reached out for help from her campus' psychological service. When she sat down with a counselor, she was a mess. She finally spoke the words she had hitherto uttered to no one.

"I had an abortion," she said.

She expected the counselor to say, "Ah-hah!" and guide her through the deep underbrush of emotions to a place where healing could begin.

He didn't. Instead there was silence, a silence she understood was meant to convey, "*So what.*"

She plummeted into deeper despair, seeking comfort through alcohol and in the arms of strangers. Since her father never gave her the affection and security a daughter needs, subconsciously she tried to obtain it through giving her body to others. It was a fool's pursuit. She would find herself scribbling the word "peace" on a scrap of paper and wonder, "*What is peace?*" She had forgotten. She would write down the words "love" and "joy," too, to the same effect.

It all culminated in 1977, six days before Christmas, when she struggled to decide whether to go home for the holidays. At the time, her father's alcoholism weighed heavily on the home like an emotional wrecking ball. She realized the awful truth that to go home would be of no consolation. Quite the opposite.

Six days before Christmas: It was her 22nd birthday. There she was, alone, fighting the temptation to end the pain and self-hatred by the only means she could think of: suicide.

Then, she clicked on the television and landed on a show called "100 Huntley Street," a Christian call-in talk show. A man was looking straight into the camera, and he asked his viewers, "Are you looking for answers? Do you want to make a change?"

Yes, and *yes*.

The man said the only path to true healing, true peace, and true meaning required the giving of our lives to Christ, and he invited viewers to call a toll-free number where counselors were standing by. Angelina dialed the number. A woman answered who, through gentle but firm persuasion, drew Angelina out into telling her story. *Everything.* It felt to Angelina like a confession.

When Angelina finished, there was a pause, and then the woman said in a compassionate voice, "Do you know what you've done is sin?"

That was the *ah-hah* moment she needed. It was her pivot point back to God.

"She called it what it was," Angelina recalls. "What a relief to call it what it was. And from there, she asked me if I was sorry for my sins and if I wanted to give my life to Jesus Christ. She asked if I was willing to forgive my father and everyone who had hurt me. And then the floodgates opened. All the unreleased tears of anger, hurt, and betrayal came pouring out. The counselor tied the abortion and all the trouble I was in to my relationship with my father, or lack thereof."

The woman then told her to turn to the Bible, to read about Jesus and His promises to the contrite, to go back to her church, whatever denomination that was, and to talk to God daily in her own words.

"Then she prayed over me, over the phone," says Angelina. "In retrospect, I now realize the Holy Spirit anointed me then and there."

As instructed, she turned to the Bible and was immediately drawn to the letters of St. Paul, who knew a thing or two about the sudden acceptance of God's grace.

Within the year, Angelina fell in love with a man who was going through his own transformation — her future husband, Walter. He had just crashed his car. She had just found God. They were two souls under repair. They married in the Church on Nov. 17, 1979. He converted to Catholicism two years later.

✝

It would be wonderful to declare they lived happily ever after. But unbeknownst to Angelina, her past was buried alive.

Before her marriage, even though she had entered the confessional to repent of her sins, she didn't *feel* absolved. She confessed her sins, she was given a penance, and that was supposed to be that. But even as she and her husband settled down together, she felt that wasn't enough. When they bought a house with enough bedrooms for a large family, she felt that wasn't it either.

When for years she was unable to conceive, she felt God was punishing her for her role in the death of the one child she was able to conceive. Despite her remorse, her guilt, and repentance — despite the fact she was beloved by all who knew her — a thought kept haunting her: "*I killed my child. How in the world could anyone ever trust me.*"

She and Walter had moved from the city to a small town in Ontario. In the city, you could be anonymous. In a small town, you could not. That's why, when she went to Mass, she would travel back to her parish in the city. There was safety in numbers. In her new town, Brooklin, Ontario, she feared — admittedly, irrationally — she would be found out as a woman who had had an abortion. In reaction, she felt herself turning to a character trait she dreaded, which was to isolate herself from others, to slink into hiding. As much as she pursued an intimate relationship with God, she still didn't quite get the message of God's mercy: that He forgives contrite sinners and that, through confession, sins are wiped clean.

In 1985, she spent the 40 days of Lent fasting to the point where she lost so much weight her clothes hardly fit her. In retrospect, she wasn't surrendering to God so much as she was punishing herself. On Good Friday, at the tiny parish in Brooklin, she went to confession and confessed the sin of her abortion for a second time. Why? Through her 40 days of fasting, she was led to a deeper awareness of the gravity of the sin of abortion.

In the confessional was a visiting priest. Apologizing to her, he said he needed to suspend the confession in order to consult with the bishop to make sure he had the authority to grant absolution in the case of abortion. He recommended she go home and wait for him to call. Stunned, Angelina went home. Through prayer that afternoon, she was given the grace to understand the indispensible role of confession — that inside the confessional, we can count on finding true solace. It's where the greatest miracles take place and where souls are transformed through God's mercy.

She felt the Blessed Virgin Mary speaking to her heart revealing the meaning of Good Friday when Christ was murdered on the cross, and how it related to her own salvation. "She was telling me how her Son, Jesus, suffered and died on the cross because of His love for all of us," Angelina says. "Our Lady watched her Son be tortured because of His love — for me. For the first time, I understood the relationship between Our Blessed Mother and Jesus and how I fit into that."

Then, the phone rang. It was the priest, and he invited her back to the confessional where, indeed, he had the power — the *responsibility* — to give her absolution.

Then, on Easter morning, the day of Jesus' Resurrection, Angelina rose from the dead, spiritually, in a way she never could have imagined. She and Walter were late for Mass because she was struggling to find clothes that would fit her. When they entered the church, it was packed and Mass was under way. She was relieved to discover she could stand in the back unnoticed. She still felt vulnerable and wished to stay out of the public eye. She felt that to step before a crowd in a church her sins would somehow be exposed. She didn't so much fear people learning of her abortion, so much as she feared them rejecting her and not loving her. But God clearly wanted her to walk down that aisle toward Him, because the priest stopped what he was doing and called Angelina and Walter to step forward to available seats in the front row.

"There is room in the Father's house for everyone," he said. The aisle was short, but the walk down it felt like a long, long, arduous journey. She imagined parishioners turning around and hissing at her, saying, "We know what you did! We know what you did!" But then, a passage from John's Gospel came flashing to her mind, when Jesus said to the crowd preparing to stone to death an adulteress, "He who is without sin among you, let him be the first to throw a stone at her" (8:7).

There is room in the Father's house for everyone.

"That's it!" she thought to herself. We are *all* sinners. This is why Jesus came down from heaven — not to minister to the righteous but to the broken-hearted. There was no one who could fall outside the mercy of God.

She took her seat and felt — *restored.*

Restored in the faith held by the girl she used to be.

✝

It gets better.

The following Sunday, her priest, Fr. Oliver Moloney, had just returned from a sabbatical where he read for the first time about a Polish nun named Sr. Maria Faustina Kowalska. He was thrilled to share with his parishioners how in a series of revelations to Sr. Faustina in the 1930s, Jesus called for a special feast day to be celebrated on the Sunday after Easter (what we know today as Divine Mercy Sunday, named by Blessed John Paul II at the canonization of St. Faustina on April 30, 2000). Quoting from a thick, red book — Faustina's *Diary* — Fr. Moloney shared some of the words Jesus spoke to Faustina:

> I desire that the Feast of Mercy be a refuge and a shelter for all souls, and especially for poor sinners. On that day the very depths of My tender mercy are open. I pour out a whole ocean of graces upon those souls who approach the fount of My mercy. The soul that will go to Confession and receive Holy Communion shall obtain complete forgiveness of

sins and punishment. On that day are opened all the divine floodgates through which graces flow. Let no soul fear to draw near to Me, even though its sins be as scarlet. ... Mankind will not have peace until it turns to the Fount of My mercy (*Diary of St. Faustina*, 699).

As she sat in the pew and listened, Angelina felt all her senses come to attention. In the days that followed, she kept turning over in her mind some of the phrases she heard:

Complete forgiveness of sins and punishment?
Let no soul fear?
Though its sins be as scarlet?

"I need to know more about this mercy he's talking about," she thought to herself.

✝

She came to understand His mercy one terrifying after-noon in 1986 — 14 difficult years after her abortion — when, again, she shouted out that one word with which she had such a tormented affiliation. The word was, "Stop."

She was on a gurney being quickly shuttled toward the operating room for emergency surgery. She was 30 years old and nearly 10 weeks pregnant. It had taken her and her husband seven years and many prayers to finally conceive. But then doctors discovered their baby was lodged in her fallopian tube, which now had ruptured. Bleeding internally and in danger of dying, she was handed a consent form to sign.

"You are pregnant," the nurse said, "but you can't keep the baby."

She signed the form before fully realizing what the nurse had said. Then, the nurses made haste to wheel her into surgery. But all the while Angelina grew increasingly unsettled.

"... but you can't keep the baby."

Is that what the nurse said?

The news of the rupture, the news of the surgery — all of it came so swiftly.

Pregnant but couldn't keep the baby. This somehow feels like an abortion is about to occur. Is this an abortion? This is an abortion. How could it not be?

"I can't do this," Angelina said, laying on her back looking up at the nurses.

"Stop," she said.

But the nurses were talking amongst themselves and hadn't heard her.

She said it again, "Stop!"

They still weren't paying attention.

In great physical pain, Angelina sat up on the gurney and yelled, "Stop!"

It was the word she used during the rape. It was the word she could not say when she was 15 years old on the abortionist's table.

The nurses stopped.

It was an incredibly empowering moment. She yelled, "Stop!" and they stopped. It felt like she had just reclaimed her free will — the free will she surrendered the night she entered that party and the afternoon she entered the abortion clinic. Isn't free will the greatest gift from God? She reclaimed it then and there — only to surrender it to God moments later.

Angelina told the nurses she wanted to see her general practitioner. When he arrived, she told him for the first time of her abortion.

"I can't go through with this unless you tell me this baby has died," she said to him. He couldn't guarantee anything other than that she would probably die if she didn't have the surgery. Angelina thought to herself that she would rather die than be responsible for the death of another child.

Walter was not there. She was alone. She could see parallels to the day she was 15 years old in the abortion clinic, but there were critical differences, too. This time, she knew she could cry out because she knew she had someone to cry out to. She turned in prayer to God — a God she was getting to know more deeply since hearing about the message of Divine Mercy by that priest at the pulpit, who quoted from that thick, red book written by a Polish nun with a funny name.

"Jesus, help. Mother Mary, help. St. Thérèse, help," Angelina cried.

It was then that "a dome of peace" enveloped her, she says. She felt a burning on her left side, and then she experienced "with spiritual eyes" the departure of the soul of her baby.

"It was my introduction to God's mercy," she says. "I had heard about His mercy, but I hadn't experienced it yet. This was my introduction."

She had the surgery. Three days in recovery, she went down into the hospital chapel. In prayer, God allowed her to see her life in its entirety, and from there, she felt she could "climb out of the pit of her sins up a ladder to His love."

Through prayer, Angelina and Walter learned their child had been a boy. They named him Joseph Michael. He had indeed died in her fallopian tube. She would learn that her abortion 14 years before had caused scar tissue to build up such that it blocked the fetus from entering her uterus. She would also learn she had what's called pelvic inflammatory disease, a sexually trans-mitted disease contracted in her younger years. For all intents and purposes, Angelina was infertile, a bitter yet fitting symbol for the culture into which she came of age.

By naming Joseph Michael, she found peace. In grieving over him, it raised the question of what had happened 14 years ago. Would it not be appropriate to name *that* child, grieve over *that* child, to admit the abortion had indeed taken the life of a child? She turned her heart to the Lord and prayed to know whether there even *was* a child and if so, was it a boy or a girl.

"The name 'Sarah Elizabeth' came to my mind, and at first I thought it was just my imagination," says Angelina. "But then I realized my prayer had been answered. I was given to know I had conceived a girl, and her name was Sarah Elizabeth. In that moment when I received her name, I received her. I restored her worth. Her life mattered. It mattered a great deal."

She and Walter would not have children. Unlike their siblings and friends, they would not experience the joy of Baptisms and graduations and grandchildren. They would be excluded from the joy of children born of love. That big house they lived in wasn't built to be so quiet.

Her abortion was supposed to prevent her from feeling excluded. That was the promise made to her way back then. The abortion, it turns out, did the opposite.

How fitting.

Terribly fitting.

✝

By July 1987, Angelina and Walter were ready to learn more about that mercy of which Fr. Moloney had talked about during that homily. They packed up a camper and embarked on a spiritual pilgrimage with the destination being a shrine they had heard about: now the "National" Shrine of The Divine Mercy in Stockbridge, Massachusetts, administered by the Marian Fathers of the Immaculate Conception, official promoters of St. Faustina's revelations since 1941. Angelina sensed that the message of Divine Mercy would answer the questions in her heart about God and forgiveness, and that it would somehow be instrumental to her in gathering up the pieces of her life and making sense of them all.

At the Shrine, she purchased a copy St. Faustina's *Diary* and found what she had been looking for since she was 15 years old. She would read of Jesus' compassion for suffering souls:

[W]hen a soul sees and realizes the gravity of its sins, when the whole abyss of the misery into which it immersed itself is displayed before its eyes, let it not despair, but with trust let it throw itself into the arms of My mercy, as a child into the arms of its beloved mother. These souls ... have first access to My mercy (1541).

She would read how Faustina gave her will over to God. In *Diary* entry 374, Faustina drew a big X across the page and declared that her own will no longer existed. In response, Jesus says: "From today on, do not fear God's judgment, for you will not be judged."

Angelina would finally understand the powerful graces God promises through the Sacrament of Reconciliation. Jesus tells St. Faustina: "When you approach the confessional, know this, that I Myself am waiting there for you. I am only hidden by the priest, but I myself act in your soul. Here the misery of the soul meets the God of mercy" (1602).

"I would read these passages," says Angelina, "and it was as though God was speaking to me, telling me, 'Do not be afraid' of Him. Despite all those assurances, He had given me since that Easter morning in 1985, I still *was* afraid of Him. I still could never imagine God being anything else but a Father who pointed a wagging finger at me. The whole message of mercy is what my soul needed to hear to be able to step out into faith and process the grief over an abortion."

The *Diary* was preparation for what would come next.

✝

God had spoken to her heart in those days following her emergency surgery. He was calling upon her. Calling upon her to do what? To gather the debris of her life — her sins, pain, grief, and disappointments. "I will take the muck and mire of your life," He spoke to her heart, "and form them into bricks and use those bricks to build My Church."

All those years pursuing God, she finally understood He was also pursuing her. She just wasn't sure what she was supposed to do. When she came upon *Diary* entry 1690, she received clarity. Jesus says to St. Faustina, "My daughter give Me souls. Know that it is your mission to win souls for Me by prayer and sacrifice, and by encouraging them to trust in My mercy."

So that was it right there: spread news of His Divine Mercy. At first, she helped coordinate Divine Mercy Sunday in her parish and the novena leading up to it. She developed and hosted Divine Mercy retreats. From those retreats, she coordinated two pilgrimages to Stockbridge — one of which was on the day of Sr. Faustina's beatification in 1993. She also would hand out for free Divine Mercy prayercards and pamphlets. She would teach people to pray the Chaplet of Divine Mercy, an intercessory prayer of conversion given to the world through St. Faustina.

All this led to her discerning a vocation within her vocation of marriage. In gathering the debris of her life, she kept recalling that Easter morning in 1985 when the priest called her and Walter to step forward before the congregation. She recalled the fear and shame she felt in doing so and how in walking down the center aisle, she had hoped she would have been able to put her abortion behind her. That Easter morning, when she was forced to step forward through her fears, God was preparing her for something. Since that morning, He had made it clear that she was not to put her abortion behind her. He had made it clear she was to step forward with courage.

That Easter morning served as a prelude to what was to come: God wanted her to go public with her abortion story, to share it with others, particularly post-abortive women and men, so that they, too, could come to realize there is room in the Father's house for everyone.

✝

In 1990, she, Walter, and Fr. Vince Heffernan, SFM, founded Second Chance Ministry, which ministers to women and men struggling with the emotional and psychological effects of abortion. The *Diary* serves as a guidebook toward healing and redemption and "nursing people back to life," Angelina says.

In addition, Angelina now serves as national coordinator in Canada for Silent No More Awareness, a non-denominational Christian public awareness and healing campaign that gathers men and women who speak out about what abortion has done to their lives.

She knows God extended His mercy to her not just for her own sake, but so that she could share it with others through works of mercy done in His name. God sends her consolations to encourage her to persevere. She has witnessed the fruits of her ministry in the lives of the many post-abortive women and men who have experienced emotional and spiritual healing, and in the love of the women who have chosen life instead of abortion.

"When I first met Angelina, she was wounded but spiritually regenerating," says Georgette Forney, co-founder of Silent No More, based in Pittsburgh, Pennsylvania. "I've since watched her become this woman of God who stepped out of her comfort zone to be the leader God has called her to be. She leads not through a place of power but through compassion and a tender heart, a servant's heart. She reflects the love of God, and that makes for a very, very powerful presence and ministry that helps bring a lot of healing to a lot of people."

Today, when Angelina stands before crowds and holds that sign saying, "I Regret My Abortion," she does so with strength — strength in the knowledge her sins are forgiven and her children are with God.

✝

Before her father's death in 2005, he had been sober for 25 years and he and Angelina had fully reconciled. She recently thumbed though his old prayer book and discovered a St. Faustina prayercard with the following passage:

> Jesus, Friend of a lonely heart, You are my haven, You are my peace. You are my salvation, You are my serenity in moments of struggle and amidst an ocean of doubts. You are the bright ray that lights up the path of my life (*Diary*, 247).

Karen Young

CHAPTER 5

Dr. Valdemar Welz

Open Wide and Say, 'Amen'

From today on, my own will
does not exist. From today on,
I do the Will of God everywhere,
always, and in everything.

— Diary of St Faustina, 374

In the Bible, the "gnashing" of teeth is a veritable dental epidemic. Seven passages in the New Testament alone speak of this grinding or grating together of the teeth. Those teeth, without exception, belonged to souls lost in a state of suffering of one form or another.

Back in 1995, a man we'll call "Harry" stepped into Dr. Valdemar Welz's dental office in Boston. Harry, 42 at the time and a successful businessman, had ground his teeth — all 28 of them — down to the gum lines. His mouth was a mess.

But he had come to the right dentist at the right time.

Dr. Welz (pronounced Wells) had just recently read the *Diary of St. Faustina*. After what he calls a "30-year search for truth," he finally found it in the *Diary*. God had suddenly become real to him. And the cause of most of the world's problems had become clear.

He took a gander at Harry's mouth. Yes, Harry would need 28 crowns, no question. "But, look, this is not a dental problem," he told Harry. "Why are you gnashing your teeth? Because of the lack of God in your life."

Harry was taken aback. Here was this dentist, one of Boston's finest, whose job entailed the science of teeth, talking about God and mercy and the power of prayer. But it paid off. Harry, a non-practicing Jew, began going to temple. With a peaceful heart — and a mended mouth — he tells people to this day that "it's all about God."

"So my first convert was Jewish!" says Dr. Welz, with a laugh.

Welcome to the world of Dr. Welz, the Divine Mercy dentist, where the motto is "brush, floss, pray, and obey."

"The *Diary* was the book that brought me back to the Catholic Church," says Dr. Welz. "When I read it that first time, it was my 'St. Thomas moment.' Think of St. Thomas after the Resurrection. Ten of his best friends told him, 'Look, the guy who walked on water, raised the dead, fed 5,000 with two fishes and five loaves, He's resurrected. We've seen Him.' And Thomas says, 'I don't believe you.'

"For 30 years, I did that. I said: 'I don't believe you.' Saint Faustina's book allowed me to put my hand in His side, my fingers in His nail holes and say, 'This is the truth.' Now, when I read the Bible, I say, 'My God, My Lord, this is the Word of God.'"

✝

It's 5:30 a.m. on a Friday in early September. Dr. Welz pulls his car up to St. Anthony's Shrine on Arch Street in Boston, as he does each weekday morning to attend Holy Mass.

The subway grates puff out stale morning breath. And about the only signs of life are a few delivery trucks that seem to wobble on arthritic knees and a couple of seagulls that circle and squawk hoarsely and half-heartedly as if they've been up all night.

Dr. Welz has been up nearly all night, too — since 1 a.m. Sleep doesn't come easily for him. In fact, his spiritual advisor orders him to sleep as an act of penance. But reading and praying do come easily. He's been reading the *Diary* for the 14th time ("Every time, I discover something different," he says). He's also been reading a book on Pope John Paul II's "Theology of the Body." ("It's a call to Divine Mercy," he says. "It's a call to imitate Christ. It's amazing!")

As for his prayer life, he's been praying for a big, long list of people — and that list always includes his beloved wife, Elzbieta, and their three children whom they adopted from Russia — Nika, Max, and Tosia.

They're all back home, sound asleep, as are most people at this hour.

Dr. Welz, with the squared-off build of a hockey player, makes his way into the Shrine, nodding to a few familiar faces he sees in the pews. The Gospel reading is Matthew 25:1-13, known as "The Ten Virgins Parable." The point of the parable is that we must prepare ourselves for Christ's coming because the stakes are high. To do otherwise means we could be left behind.

This, of course, is right up Dr. Welz's alley, and he nods knowingly.

Through his attempt of trying to preserve his patients' teeth for a lifetime, he does everything he can to get their souls into heaven. That is to say, he fights tooth decay and *truth* decay. And the *Diary*— the reading of which he frequently "prescribes" for his patients — contains precisely the very truth that the world needs now more than ever, he says. The truth being that God is with us, that He is merciful above all else, and that we must turn to Him in trust.

"What I do for people in the office is I say, 'Can I give you a present?' Who can refuse a present? Most of the time, the gift I give them is the *Diary*," he says. "I give them away. I mean, what do they cost? Eight bucks? Eight bucks to save a soul?"

✝

After Mass, he heads to a coffee shop, buys a coffee, and steers his car toward his office. It's located in Boston's posh Back Bay, where the handsome and historic townhouses sit straight and snug, like sets of perfect teeth.

Today, perfect teeth are not on his agenda. It's Friday, his favorite day. Why? Because each Friday he reserves time for his non-paying patients — people referred to him who are most in need, as well as to religious, including sisters from St. Faustina's order who live in Boston and members of the Marian Fathers of the Immaculate Conception.

It's not a lopsided relationship, Dr. Welz admits. He puts them "to work," as he says.

"Whenever I come, he has a list for me," says Very Rev. Fr. Kazimierz Chwalek, MIC, the Marians' provincial superior in the United States and Argentina. "Sometimes, he wants me to talk to people on the phone whom he's met who need spiritual counseling. He takes these things seriously. He wants to provide people in need with ministerial resources."

"One thing is for sure," says Fr. Seraphim Michalenko, MIC, a renowned expert on the life and spirituality of St. Faustina and a patient of Dr. Welz, "he doesn't want anyone to go to hell."

Until Divine Mercy Sunday in 2006, atop Dr. Welz's list of people in need was his own brother, Roman, who served as his associate for decades. Roman had been diagnosed with pancreatic cancer in 2005. By April 2006, he was clearly dying. Dr. Welz urged him on many occasions to consult with a priest, but Roman brushed the notion aside.

Then, on the eve of Divine Mercy Sunday in 2006, Dr. Welz prayed the Chaplet of the Divine Mercy for his brother with the special intention that Roman would go to heaven. The next day, unbeknownst to Dr. Welz at the time, Roman received the Sacraments of the Church. He then died on July 29, 2006.

Roman's name remains on the door of the dentistry office "as a reminder to me of what my goal in life is," says Dr. Welz, "— to get to heaven."

In his eulogy at Roman's funeral, Dr. Welz laid out a plan on how everyone can join Roman in heaven.

"What is the purpose of life?" he said. "To get to heaven. How do we do that? We have to become saints. How do we become saints? By imitating Jesus."

✝

Dr. Welz wasn't always like this. Born in Poland, raised in Boston, he had, from an early age, an inclination to question the things that were presented to him as absolute truth. And that included his Catholic faith. When he was 14 and in CCD class, he asked so many questions that the priest who was his teacher finally stormed out of the room.

That marked the beginning of a 30-year period in which he all but closed the door on Catholicism. But during that period, he read everything he could get his hands on — philosophy books, spiritual books, psychology books — searching for meaning.

Finally, in 1994, in a book of quotes, he came across this one, "It's all about forgiveness." For the dentist, that touched a nerve. He formulated a theory — that God, in effect, is asking us to forgive everyone who has ever hurt us. Then, at the same time, through His mercy, He forgives us for everything we've ever done that's sinful.

Several months later, in the spring of 1995, his dental hygienist, Christine Schneider, a Divine Mercy devotee, handed him a copy of the *Diary of St. Faustina*, a book written in the 1930s by the Polish nun that includes revelations she received from Jesus Christ.

That was a Thursday. He spent the entire weekend "devouring" it, he says.

His former CCD teacher might be pleased to know that Dr. Welz no longer has any questions about God. They've all been answered, he says.

"But I'm sure God has lots of questions for me," he says, with a laugh.

✝

At 7:40 a.m., a young Polish immigrant named Malgorzata is first in the dentist chair. She needs a filling. But first thing's first. Dr. Welz, dressed now in green scrubs with a Divine Mercy pin, clicks on the office music — not the typical Muzak, but rather the Psalms in song.

Because of dental dams and other sorts of obtrusive instrumentation, most patients' mouths are often too occupied to join in any conversation. So Dr. Welz typically has the floor, so to speak.

"Do you know why Valdemar has two dental assistants?" Kasia, one of his dental assistants, asks. "To make sure he's not talking the whole time." She's teasing him. "We point to our watches. We wave our hands," she says, with a smile.

He's talking to Malgorzata about the *Diary* now. Specifically paragraph 374 in which St. Faustina crosses out her will and writes, "From today on, my own will does not exist. From today on, I do the Will of God everywhere, always, and in everything."

"Amazing, isn't it?" he says, pulling his facemask down around his neck. "The most powerful thing we can do," he says, "is give our wills totally over to God. It's an amazing thing, and it's only then when you realize how wonderful and merciful God is."

Can all this zeal be overbearing for some patients? It's a question that's not new to Dr. Welz. He's given it a lot of thought. His spiritual advisor acknowledges, "I have to channel his enthusiasm from time to time." But Dr. Welz likens himself to the bartender who talks baseball, or a barber who talks politics. With candor, humor, and conviction — and in between drilling and filling teeth — he holds court inside his elegantly appointed office at 398 Commonwealth Avenue, talking with his patients and 12-member staff about Divine Mercy.

"How could I not discuss this with people?" he says. "That's insane. God is the most important thing in my life."

He pauses. Then, he adds, "People want to hear the truth. They yearn for it."

No one can argue with that. Plus, his business is booming. He's booked solid several months in advance.

By day's end, he's performed half a dozen procedures, including a root canal on a low-income mother. He's also given the Catholic chaplain of New England Medical Center a new gold crown and gold inlay (what Dr. Welz jokingly referred to as a "chalice" and a "paten").

At 4 p.m., the babysitter drops off his three children. He lets them make "super balls" out of lab putty while he finishes up his work. Then, they all pile into the car excitedly. It's Friday. They're going to meet their mother at home and have a feast. The children have headphones on. They're snapping their gum (sugar-free, of course).

"OK, kids," Dr. Welz says, as he twists the key and starts the car. "What's the purpose of life?"

They stop what they're doing and respond in unison: "To get to heaven!"

A wide smile takes over his face as he puts the car in drive.

Felix Carroll

CHAPTER 6

Joe Walker

A Model of Mercy Emerges from a Grisly Killing

Jesus to St Faustina:
If a soul does not exercise mercy
somehow or other, it will not obtain
My mercy on the day of judgment.

– Diary of St Faustina, 1317

Second pew to the left. Last seat to the left. That's where Joseph Walker prays for the soul of his daughter and for the man who murdered her.

It's the closest seat to the image of the Divine Mercy at St. William the Confessor Church in Greenville, Texas. In the image, Jesus' gaze is penetrating. To Mr. Walker, He seems to be saying, "*You know I am real, you know I love you, and you know what to do.*"

"Jesus doesn't turn anyone away," Mr. Walker says, his eyes trained on the image after all the parishioners have gone, following Holy Mass on a humid autumn morning in 2012. Mr. Walker doesn't turn anyone away either. Moments later, he's walking through the parish hall. He moves slower now. Stage-three kidney disease keeps him bent over and fatigued.

In a closet in the hall, he stores a supply of Divine Mercy materials he purchases to give out free. Over the years — ever since the message of Divine Mercy and the *Diary of St. Faustina* changed his life — Mr. Walker has given out tens of thousands of pamphlets and prayercards and several hundred copies of the *Diary of St. Faustina.*

Ishmael, the office assistant, tells him he is putting together school supplies for poor Hispanic youth. The supplies will includes pens, pencils, notebooks, and whatever else is available.

"Give them a *Diary*, too. I've got a box coming in any day now," Mr. Walker says as he walks toward the door. He pauses by the doorway before he steps back out into the scorching heat, and he adds, "Everyone needs a *Diary*."

"It's a love story," he says of the *Diary*, once outside the parish hall, "of St. Faustina's love of Jesus, and Jesus' love for all of us."

By "all," he means *all*. Everyone. Including those who commit unspeakable acts of violence.

✝

Years earlier, on July 8, 2006, Mr. Walker had returned home from confession when he found a note on his door. It was from the police. They wanted to speak to him as soon as possible.

When the police arrived, they told him the news. His daughter, Sarah Anne Walker, a 40-year-old mother of two, had been brutally murdered. Her body was discovered inside a model home in a new residential development in Texas, north of Dallas, where Ms. Walker worked as a real estate agent.

The crime drew national attention as investigators searched for the killer. It was featured on cable news networks and on the program "America's Most Wanted." The attention helped investigators track down the killer. It also helped Mr. Walker get an important message out through the mainstream media — a message of mercy. From the outset, a number of news outlets reported that Mr. Walker prays the Chaplet of the Divine Mercy every day not only for the repose of the soul of his daughter but for her killer as well.

"This murder devastated my whole family," says Mr. Walker, a retired retail executive who lives in Greenville, "but Divine Mercy is what's gotten my family through this."

Sarah Anne was the oldest of three children born to Mr. Walker and his wife, Carol. Family and friends say she always seemed happy and hopeful. When she was a child, her father traveled a lot, and she would miss him dearly. So much so that, while only in grammar school, she read a copy of one of her father's favorite books at the time, *The Greatest Salesman in the World*, by Og Mandino. She wanted to impress him. The book is a treatise on the philosophy and spirituality of salesmanship. Among the many words of wisdom is "... do not aspire for wealth and labor not only to be rich. Strive instead for happiness, to be loved and to love, and most important to acquire peace of mind and serenity."

The message took. She would grow to live by those words and to make her father proud.

"She was full of life, a beautiful young lady, and quite renowned in the real estate business," says Mr. Walker. She adored her two children and was always so considerate when it came to her parents.

He shared how the day before her murder, Sarah Anne wrote him an e-mail about her visit just days before. She had brought her 4-year-old son, Josh, and niece Kendyl over to spend time with their grandmother, who was seriously ill at the time and who continues to suffer from major health problems.

"I promise you that for those two hours, Josh and Kendyl were praying for Mom ... the angels heard them," Sarah Anne wrote. "I let Mom know that we are going to bring Kendyl and Josh back out next Thursday to see her again."

But her murder prevented that.

Investigators say a couple looking at a model home discovered Sarah Anne's body.

"The FBI says it was one of the most brutal single murders they had ever investigated," Mr. Walker says. "He stabbed her 27 times. Bashed her skull in. She had bite marks on her. It was senseless. It was a horrible, horrible crime."

No motive for the murder was announced, but police say Ms. Walker's Rolex watch and ring were stolen.

While Mr. Walker recalls the shock he and his family felt after learning of Sarah Anne's killing, close friends of the Walkers were not shocked by the reaction of Mr. Walker, who immediately leaned on his faith. A member of the Knights of Columbus, Mr. Walker is well known in his parish for his corporal and spiritual works of mercy.

In addition to giving out copies of the *Diary of St. Faustina*, prayercards, and Divine Mercy images that he has framed, he is known as the man who buys and serves doughnuts and other treats after Mass and at other parish events. Admittedly, he does so mostly to entice the children. Maybe that's not "proper" — maybe it's bribery — but he was a successful businessman, after all. In some matters of business, the most important thing is the bottom line. In this case, the bottom line is to help foster a new generation of joyful Catholics. If it takes doughnuts, then it takes doughnuts.

He's also the man to whom many people turn when a loved one is on their deathbed. They know Mr. Walker will pray the Chaplet of the Divine Mercy for them.

"He would never tell you this stuff. He's too humble," says his pastor, Fr. Paul Weinberger.

Father Paul recalls the first clue people got of how the Walkers were handling the murder of Sarah Anne. Father Paul was just about to lead mourners in the Rosary at the funeral home when Mr. Walker interrupted and said to all those gathered, "And we've got to pray for the one who did this."

It was a natural reaction, and one he stands by to this day.

"Remember what Jesus said of His tormentors and killers when He was dying on the cross. He said, 'Father, forgive them, for they do not know what they are doing,'" said Mr. Walker, quoting from the Gospel of St. Luke, 23:34. "If you don't abide by that, you don't stand a chance."

The Gospel message is echoed in St. Faustina's *Diary*, in which Jesus calls humanity to a deeper understanding that God's love is unlimited and available to everyone. "The greater the sinner, the greater the right he has to My mercy," Jesus told St. Faustina (*Diary*, 723).

"If you study the *Diary of St. Faustina*," says Mr. Walker, "you learn that you have to show mercy and forgive in order to *receive* mercy."

"Joe was just so insistent that the killer not be left out — that it be public," said Fr. Paul. "The way he comported himself with the murder of his daughter — it showed that his faith is not just something superficial. It's deep."

Born in 1943 and raised in Dubuque, Iowa, Mr. Walker struggled from an early age. Both his parents died when he was young. Polio kept him bedridden for two years. By the time he graduated high school, he weighed less than 100 pounds. He and his wife met in the sandbox in elementary school and married on Thanksgiving Day in 1964. Most of Carol's adult life has been spent battling illness. Despite everything, Mr. Walker doesn't recall shedding a tear until he watched the movie *The Passion of the Christ*.

"When the Roman soldiers started hitting Him, beating Him, I just cried for them to stop," he says.

He was spiritually prepared to watch *The Passion* because, through the *Diary of St. Faustina*, he first came to understand Jesus' greatest attribute, which is mercy. When he was first handed a copy of the *Diary* in the year 2000 — incidentally, the year St. Faustina was canonized — he put it down only to sleep. He read the whole thing in two days.

He was struck most by the promises Jesus makes to those who pray the chaplet, which he prays at least once a day. Jesus told St. Faustina:

> Whoever will recite [the chaplet] will receive great mercy at the hour of death (687). When they say this chaplet in the presence of the dying, I will stand between My Father and the dying person, not as the just Judge but as the Merciful Savior (1541). Priests will recommend it to sinners as their last hope of salvation. Even if there were a sinner most hardened, if he were to recite this chaplet only once, he would receive grace from My infinite mercy (687). I desire to grant unimaginable graces to those souls who trust in My mercy (687). Through the chaplet you will obtain everything, if what you ask for is compatible with My will (1731).

He said the *Diary* transformed him from a "lukewarm Catholic." He led a sinful life, he says. "I was a son of a gun. And it brought to mind all the times I spit in Jesus' face, too, like those Roman soldiers, and all the times I put that crown of thorns on Him."

What was it about the message of Divine Mercy that touched him so?

"I've learned through the message of Divine Mercy that no prayers go to waste — ever," Mr. Walker says. "You may not have confidence in your prayers, but they don't go to waste. And I've learned that God never sends you any more than you can handle. I know that, and I trust in that. I've learned that we must pray, pray, pray. It never ceases to work," he says. "I know the Chaplet of the Divine Mercy works. I know that if you practice everything that St. Faustina mentions in her *Diary* that you will have an outstanding chance of going to heaven. Divine Mercy saved my life. It saved my wife's life."

Abiding trust in the Lord served as the inspiration for Fr. Paul's homily a week following the murder of Sarah Anne.

"You see, Joe has a great devotion to the Divine Mercy," Fr. Paul told parishioners. "And year after year, hour after hour, Joe has prayed the Divine Mercy Chaplet. And if mercy is what you want, mercy is what you have to give. Joe could say those words soon after his dear daughter had been murdered, and he was saying them in all honesty. He wasn't saying them through clenched teeth. He didn't say he hoped God had mercy on the *fiend*, *coward*, or *wretch* who did this to his daughter.

"It is amazing," Fr. Paul continued. "Divine Mercy had prepared Joe for that moment."

Kosoul Chanthakoummane, a Laotian immigrant who had no connection with Sarah Anne, was convicted of her murder. He had previously served seven years of an 11-year sentence for two counts each of aggravated kidnapping and aggravated robbery. Against Mr. Walker's wishes, the Collin County District Attorney's Office successfully sought the death penalty for Mr. Chanthakoummane, who was 25 years old at the time of the murder. Now, on death row in Livingston, Texas, Mr. Chanthakoummane was sentenced to die by lethal injection for the murder.

"There's no reason they cannot give him life without parole," says Mr. Walker, who has never met Mr. Chanthakoummane. "To put him to death and to take another life — I don't think our Lord would want that. So that's the next fight I'm gearing up for. People want revenge, but revenge never works. Yes, it was just a totally senseless, random act. But everyone deserves every bit of their life, so they can have a chance to repent and go to heaven. I believe that totally, completely.

"God wants to not lose even *one* soul," Mr. Walker continues. "He wants all with Him in His heavenly kingdom."

Though enduring days of pure agony during the trial in October 2007, Mr. Walker would post a daily message from the *Diary* on the *Semper Fi* Catholic web forum. The passages included:

My Jesus, You know that from my earliest years I have wanted to become a great saint; that is to say, I have wanted to love You with a love so great that there would be no soul who has hitherto loved You so (*Diary*, 1372).

[Concerning His Sacred Heart, Jesus speaks to Sister Faustina:] "My Heart is mercy itself" (*Diary*, 1777).

[God listens to holy souls:] I am striving for sanctity, because in this way I shall be useful to the Church (*Diary*, 1505).

On the final day of the trial, he wrote to Mr. Chanthakoummane's family explaining how he prays the Divine Mercy Chaplet every day for him. He also wrote them that he forgives Mr. Chanthakoummane completely. He put the letter in an envelope with a copy of the *Diary* and several Divine Mercy pamphlets.

Back at his favorite seat at St. William the Confessor Catholic Church, Mr. Walker explains what he will do on the day Mr. Chanthakoummane will be put to death.

"If I am still alive, I'll go down to the prison and make a big scene," he says.

If he were to ever meet the man who killed his daughter, what would he say to him?

"I told him through the newspapers that I forgive him," Mr. Walker says. "I truly do. I would say to him in person, 'I hope in your heart you could really understand our Lord loves you.' That would be it."

He has sent Mr. Chanthakoummane a copy of the *Diary*. He has not heard back.

But on his death row webpage profile, Mr. Chanthakoummane wrote, "*I pray God's mercy on my soul.*"

Felix Carroll

CHAPTER 7

Terry Muzones

'Nothing to Fear'

I desire that my whole life be but one act of thanksgiving to You, O God.

— Diary of St. Faustina, 1285

She won't take the bait.

The Arrivals and Departures sign inside Albany International Airport shows that a plane will leave for Fort Lauderdale, Florida, in 35 minutes.

Would she ever consider a vacation to a sunny resort town to chill out for a few days? Maybe drink a piña colada on a white, sandy beach?

"Absolutely not," Terry Muzones says, with a laugh.

A flight leaves in 90 minutes for Las Vegas, Nevada. How about trying her luck on the slots?

She laughs, "No."

A flight to Tucson, Arizona, leaves in two hours. What about getting a deep-muscle massage in a froufrou desert spa?

"Nope."

Just testing.

Of course, these options are absurd. Terry's job with the airline industry comes with an invaluable perk: close to free air travel. But vacations aren't her thing. Relaxing is not her thing. She can't even watch a television program without also paying bills or returning e-mails at the same time.

She's in Albany, New York, now on a layover on her way home to Illinois. A jetsetter for the Lord, she carves out vacation time and long weekends to hop on planes to foreign destinations — Africa, Europe, and Asia, including Communist China — where she visits Catholic parishes and schools. During these visits, she speaks about the message of Divine Mercy as revealed to St. Faustina in the 1930s. She teaches how to apply the message of Divine Mercy in daily life, and how to practice the corporal and spiritual works of mercy. She helps form prayer groups — called cenacles —that focus on Scripture, the *Catechism of the Catholic Church*, the *Diary of St. Faustina*. She also teaches those within the groups how to pray the Chaplet of the Divine Mercy.

"You can feel her genuineness of spirit, her love for the Eucharist in bonding with the Divine Mercy," says Malou Pimentel, of the Netherlands, who started a cenacle following a visit by Terry. "I am thankful for her firsthand testimony, which widened my horizon in learning about the wondrous works of the Divine Mercy."

Why all the tens of thousands of miles annually in the name of mercy? This is her way of giving back to God for all the blessings and graces she and her family have received over the years.

She has just returned from Uganda in Africa, where, among other commitments on her busy evangelical itinerary, she led a seminar attended by 200 people representing 52 parishes in the Masaka Diocese. During this trip in fall 2012, Bishop John Baptist Kaggwa stayed for the entire seven-hour seminar and took notes, as did a brigadier general of the Ugandan Army and a member of the Ugandan Parliament.

"The fruits of the seminar," says Terry, "was when Bishop John Baptist officially announced at the end of the seminar his decision to implement the formation of the cenacle on the Divine Mercy in all the 52 parishes under him. It was a very productive visit, and I could have easily stayed two more weeks and kept myself busy. Maybe another time."

Maybe?

Probably.

Oh, and on the way back from Uganda, she stopped in Europe to visit her daughter and arranged to make a trip back to that region "to target some of the students and parishioners in Leuven, Belgium."

She hopes to get a Divine Mercy cenacle developed there, too.

"I trust that Jesus will lead the way for me to follow," she says.

The author and popular speaker Fr. Donald Calloway, MIC, gives great credit to the role Catholic Filipino women played in his powerful religious conversion, calling them "God's super agents that He places all over the earth."

Diminutive, devout, a dynamo, Terry Muzones fits the description. But before becoming a super agent of God, she was a super stressed-out workaholic. Like many immigrants to the United States, she pursued the American dream of freedom — freedom amplified by prosperity and success and making a better life for her family. Her career success came as no surprise to anyone.

From the province of Iloilo, in the Philippines, Terry was a go-getter from the beginning. She graduated college at the tender age of 17. Then, she spent two years teaching college students who were her seniors by several years. Though her parents weren't churchgoers, they served as role models — industrious as much as they were charitable. They grew coconuts, coffee, and fruit trees, and raised cattle for meat on a large tract of land. They also owned a fleet of commercial fishing boats. All the while, they ensured their neighbors would never go hungry. Once, when a fishing boat from a rival fleet capsized, Terry's mother fed those families until the Red Cross could provide assistance.

Terry and her five siblings would grow up to live by their parents' example. But they would also grow up to witness the government move in and confiscate the family's land without providing compensation. That ordeal would make a mark on Terry in her later life when she would amass material wealth and guard it with an attentiveness that sometimes bordered on obsession. God would eventually cure her of that when the time was right.

In 1968, in her early 20s, during what was supposed to be a two-month visit to the United States, Terry decided to stay put and get a green card. Her boyfriend from the Philippines, Rafael, eventually joined up with her in Chicago where they married and had two children together. Six years later, she escorted Rafael's body back home to the Philippines after he was killed in a car accident.

Suddenly, a single mother to a five- and three-year-old, Terry declined her parents' offer to care for the children in the Philippines. Instead, she brought her children with her back to Chicago, where she leaned into the head winds of hard times to bear witness to the power of a mother's love.

She had no financial support and no savings. For years, this was her schedule:

- Wake at 5 a.m. and get her children fed and packed.

- Drop them off to the babysitter, who lived in the same low-income apartment building as Terry.

- Get to her secretarial job at a law office at 8 a.m.

- Hop on the subway at 5 p.m. to her job at Sears, where she worked as a clerk.

- Leave that job at 9 p.m. and take the subway to the *Chicago Tribune*, where she worked as an operator until midnight.

- Arrive back at the babysitter's at 1 a.m. Carry her two sleeping children one by one from the babysitter's to their beds and tuck them in.

She'd start all over again at 5 a.m.

Ten years after the birth of her first child, Terry was in a relationship and had two more children. Eventually, she moved to the suburbs and had a good-paying job working as a researcher for a pharmaceutical company. She made sure she took her children to Mass on Sundays, and during this time, she felt drawn more and more into a relationship with God. But she always felt that poverty was chasing her down, which only motivated her to work harder, longer hours.

She wound up landing a job for a major credit card company and was promoted to an account executive position. Terry became a huge success, but because her earnings were based almost entirely on commissions, she was barely home, and when she was, usually she was making sales calls. She hardly slept. On one hand, she earned enough money to put all four of her children through school and to provide them with a comfortable life — no small feat. But on the other hand, she felt she could rarely give her full attention to people who were not business associates.

Her motivation had become myopically money oriented. She had allowed friends to fall by the wayside. Even her brothers and sisters rarely called because whenever they reached out to her, Terry would be irritated. She would usually be "in the middle of something," with no time to talk.

"It was awful," she says. "I was so wrapped up in my career every day and all the time. Everything else became a distraction."

In 1998, Terry needed a vacation, so she packed her bags and took her two youngest daughters to Medjugorje, in the former Yugoslavia, the popular pilgrimage site where six people have reported receiving apparitions of the Virgin Mary since 1981. (The Catholic Church has not made a final ruling on the authenticity of the alleged apparitions there.) She was curious, and she hoped the trip might afford her a chance for prayerful decompression.

While Medjugorje was more commercialized than she had imagined, Terry eventually loosened up and allowed herself to temporarily forget her work and career. It was then that she experienced a profound presence of Jesus banging at the door of her heart. Alone at 5 a.m. in a field, kneeling at the foot of the cross near the site of the reported Marian apparitions, she received the grace to know Jesus was real and that He sought to live in her heart and change her life.

"At one moment, I felt I wanted to die because I knew I would be with Jesus," she says. "I felt complete. It changed everything. I felt so much love for Him and from Him, and I knew there was nothing more on earth to live for."

Old habits die hard. Upon her return to the United States, Terry snapped back to the cold reality of her all-consuming career. But that didn't last long. One morning when she awoke, she looked in the mirror and didn't like what she saw.

"I realized I had become an ugly person," she says. "I had isolated myself from everyone. I had isolated myself from God, too. I knew it was time to give back to God what He had given my family and me. I knew money is not the only thing that's important, and it was time to serve the Lord."

In a shocking decision — to her bosses and even to herself — Terry quit her job. Unknown to what God's plan was for her, she landed a job with the airline industry, but at a fraction of her salary with the credit card company. It was a leap of faith. She did it with trepidation. But with her children grown, she knew it was time to reprioritize. God's future "super agent" was now a "super contrite" child of God. Holy Mass and the Sacraments replaced a fat paycheck in her ledger of things that motivated her. But before Terry could truly declare herself fit to serve God with all her heart, she would need to let her "yes" be "yes," and her "no" be "no," as the Gospel of Matthew teaches. "For whatever is more than these is from the evil one" (5:37).

Her faith was tested when Terry suffered a house fire that started in her kitchen when a friend was cooking. The fire nearly destroyed her home, and she and her family were displaced for eight months. Years later, she suffered another blow. She had accrued a fortune in jewelry over the years — enough jewelry that she easily could have opened a small jewelry store.

"I had 6.5 carat diamonds," she says now, still rather amazed.

She kept her jewelry in a closet locked inside a heavy steel safe. One day, robbers broke into her home and stole the entire safe. She was robbed blind.

But as we know, Christ gives sight to the blind.

☩

Over lunch during her Albany layover, Terry says the robbery traumatized her in two ways. First, the monetary and sentimental loss was enormous. Those jewels represented the fruits of her hard labor and proof of how her resolve to rise above poverty had paid off. Secondly, the robbery brought to light an uncomfortable truth. Clearly, despite all her talk of surrender to God, she still attached herself to the unnecessary things of the world. The robbery caused her to divest herself of superfluous material things.

She knew in her heart to guard herself against all covetousness. From her childhood in Catholic school, she knew from the words of Matthew's Gospel that she was not to store up "treasures on earth, where moth and rust destroy, and where thieves break in and steal. But store up for yourselves treasures in heaven " (6 :19-20). How amazingly ironic: "thieves," Matthew uses the word "*thieves.*"

God can be so literal.

She moved out of the house for good, settling in a home that serves as a symbol of her new life. The only jewelry she owns now is a watch. She now checks it: It's 90 minutes until her plane leaves for Chicago.

☦

Looking back at her ordeals, beginning with the death of her husband, Terry learned during this time to be thankful. Yes, *thankful.* That's because she finally came to understand what thankfulness meant. She learned its definition when she cracked open a thick, red book she had laying around but had never read, called the *Diary of St. Faustina.* Among the many spiritual insights she gained were these words written on Nov. 5, 1934, when Sr. Faustina, a Polish nun and mystic, recorded an astounding passage about being thankful to God:

> True love is measured by the thermometer of suffering. Jesus, I thank You for the little daily crosses, for opposition to my endeavors, for the hardships of communal life, for the misinterpretation of my intentions, for humiliations at the hands of others, for the harsh way in which we are treated, for false suspicions, for poor health and loss of strength, for self-denial, for dying to myself, for lack of recognition in everything, for the upsetting of all my plans.

Thank You, Jesus, for interior suffering, for dryness of spirit, for terrors, fears, and incertitudes, for the darkness and the deep interior night, for temptations and various ordeals, for torments too difficult to describe, especially for those which no one will understand, for the hour of death with its fierce struggle and all its bitterness.

I thank You, Jesus, You who first drank the cup of bitterness before You gave it to me, in a much milder form. I put my lips to this cup of Your holy will. Let all be done according to Your good pleasure; let that which Your wisdom ordained before the ages be done to me. I want to drink the cup to its last drop, and not seek to know the reason why. In bitterness is my joy, in hopelessness is my trust. In You, O Lord, all is good, all is a gift of Your paternal Heart. I do not prefer consolations over bitterness or bitterness over consolations, but thank You, O Jesus, for everything! (343)

Terry's first impression of this passage was, "*Wow!*" Here was St. Faustina, in her darkest hours, in the midst of untold humiliations, sufferings, and scotched plans, and what emotion does she express? Thankfulness. "How does she *do* that?" wondered Terry. First, it helped Terry to realize that the *Diary* serves as an instruction manual to build holiness — a sometimes frustrating and complicated assembly project. Did Terry have the necessary parts, so to speak? For instance, did she have the capacity for thankfulness in times of darkness, loss, humiliation, and blows to her ego?

Like many half-assembled pilgrims making their way on this planet, she sometimes felt tempted to say, "*Thanks for nothing!*" Yet, she realized God was challenging her to understand that to be truly united with Him as saints like Faustina were, our only sane response is, "*Thanks for everything!*" She realized that without God we are sorry sights — limping, lost, wandering, and half blind. Once we realize this, we, too, can be God's friend, thankful for Him in our lives, in good times and bad.

Terry realized that, out of His love for us, God sent His Son to find us. His Son offered His life on the cross as a reward to bring us home. It matters not how flawed we are. It matters not where we've been and what we've done. Saint Faustina taught Terry that only in our thankfulness does true earthly joy reside and that only in His love for us can we find the heavenly harvest that truly strengthens our souls.

He wants us back — broken, imperfect, and half-blind though we are.

Since then, Terry's desire is that, in the words of St. Faustina, her whole life "be but one act of thanksgiving to You, O God" (*Diary*, 1285).

"Terry is a very special lady to sacrifice and travel halfway around the world to tell others of God's mercy," says Dr. Bryan Thatcher, founder of Eucharistic Apostles of The Divine Mercy (EADM). "She is bearing great fruit, and the message of mercy is falling on ears that are open to listen. Bishops support her and appreciate all she does. EADM continues its worldwide growth due to people like her."

It is under the auspices of EADM that Terry helps start cenacles and give talks around the world. EADM is a lay apostolate of the Congregation of Marian Fathers of the Immaculate Conception, official Divine Mercy promoters since 1941. With close to free airfare, Terry also serves as a volunteer at the National Shrine of The Divine Mercy in Stockbridge, Massachusetts — 850 miles from home.

Most of her evangelization is conducted far away from Chicago. Why? She finds that people in places such as Africa and Asia hunger for Divine Mercy more so than in the United States.

"We live such a comfortable life here," she says. "Many people here don't realize they need God. It's like pulling teeth. I just feel like I can do more for God and His kingdom in places where people realize how much they need Him."

The message of Divine Mercy, she says, serves as the greatest instrument to bring people closer to God because

"Jesus speaks so clearly through St. Faustina about His love for us, no matter what our sins have been. Some people still believe that sin is a barrier to God, and it isn't."

Terry also teaches the importance of offering prayers, works, and sacrifices for the Holy Souls in Purgatory in order to help release them into heaven. She honors as well a promise she made to the Blessed Virgin Mary to teach people to pray the Rosary of Seven Sorrows, as Our Lady requested in her apparitions in the 1980s in Kibeho, Rwanda.

Closer to home, Terry volunteers at Marytown's St. Maximilian Kolbe Prison Ministry where they provide free Bibles and other religious materials to inmates. She is in her final year before profession into the *Ordo Franciscanus Saecularis*, the Third Order Franciscans. She also has her own ministry of providing home enthronements to the Divine Mercy by bringing a two-foot Divine Mercy statue into people's homes. When she delivers the statue, she stands with the families and offers the following prayer:

> As you welcome Jesus into your home and trust in His Divine Mercy, you will be filled with an abundance of graces that you can spread to others. Let us make it our mission to bring the Divine Mercy into each family and to put into practice the corporal and spiritual works of mercy for the greater glory of God.

She put that prayer to paper, which stays with the statue should it be passed along without her assistance. The statue stays in each house for a few days, and then it's passed on to another family, and on and on.

"The last I saw it was two years ago," says Terry. "I think it's somewhere in Buffalo now."

She laughs.

"That's okay," she says. "I'm sure it's serving the purpose that God intends."

She looks down again at the only piece of jewelry she owns. It's time for her to go. Her flight leaves in 45 minutes.

"I just want to teach people to pray," she says. "If we have God in our hearts, He leads us to where we are going. He wants us to go, ultimately, back to Him."

For Terry, it's back to Illinois.

She gathers her purse and travel bag. The bag is tiny, big enough to fit a change of clothes, the Bible, the *Diary of St. Faustina*, and little else.

"I think God wanted me to be just a simple person," she says, bidding adieu before she passes through security and boards her plane to Chicago — cold this time of year, definitely not vacationland.

CHAPTER 8

Dr. John Bruchalski

'A Second Pentecost'

Jesus to St. Faustina:

Mankind will not have peace until it turns with trust to My mercy.

— Diary of St Faustina, 300

In a crowded assembly room at the University of Arizona College of Medicine in Phoenix, a kindly, young medical student clicks on the wireless microphone to introduce the guest speaker. Reading carefully from a cue card, she says the talk is titled "The Hypocrisy Factor."

"We hope this will be a valuable discussion," she says. "Nothing is off-limits in terms of topics of discussion, so please open up your hearts and minds, and hopefully this will be a topic everyone will learn from."

Meanwhile, the guest speaker, Dr. John Bruchalski, is in the background pacing like a football coach who wears a headset and takes advice from his offensive coordinator high up in the booth. In a manner of speaking, Dr. Bruchalski is on the offensive, and he does receive his direction from on high — from Jesus, the Blessed Mother, and the Communion of Saints. But this is *definitely* not the venue to go into any of that. Suffice it to say, he's pacing, and he's sipping bottled water and clearing his throat as the kindly student cites his credentials: He's an obstetrician/gynecologist. ... University of South Alabama College of Medicine. ... Eastern Virginia School of Medicine. ... Founder of the Tepeyac Family Center and chairman of Divine Mercy Care in northern Virginia. A father of two boys ...

As he awaits his turn at the microphone, Dr. Bruchalski — dressed in a blue blazer and a pair of khakis that could have used an ironing — looks equal parts nervous and exhausted. He's just flown in from the University of Texas in Houston, where he delivered a similar talk, and before that, Indiana for the same reason. He's still getting used to the fact that his audience these days is not comprised mostly of elderly, pro-life Catholics who pretty much already know the gist of what they will hear: a powerful conversion story, a bold effort to care for the disenfranchised, and an indictment of the nation's medical industry. Instead, they are mostly young, idealistic, well-learned, book-bag toting, curious, thoughtful future medical professionals, many of whom are sitting attentively and wondering what in the world they will hear from this visiting doctor whose pro-life views precede him.

When he does take the microphone and begins, he knows for certain the words he will *not* utter. He will not say the words God, Jesus, Holy Spirit, Our Lady, Divine Mercy, or salvation. He might not even say the word compassion. He's a God-loving, God-fearing man — and he's also not stupid. By framing an argument in those terms to a crowd with a course load that includes such subjects as systems-based histology, or left ventricular dynamics and pathophysiology, chances are fantastically high that he would instantly be dismissed as a "religious fanatic" with a "religious agenda." What would be the point? Sad but true: That's how much religion has been marginalized in this country.

Anyway, he doesn't need to use those words to get his point across. He's not here to convert them. He gladly yields to the Holy Spirit on that score. He's here to speak to these students in "*their* language," as he puts it, using data, reason, even left-leaning journalism, and, of course, firsthand experience.

Dr. Bruchalski is a former abortionist. His speaking tour was arranged by National Med Students for Life, a group that by all accounts has not been marginalized on medical college campuses. With a future that will likely include scalpels and all manner of invasive surgery as well as fearful and emotional patients, these students seem to take nothing for granted.

"I've been on both sides of this issue," Dr. Bruchalski tells the students. "I initially went into residency to liberate women from the chains of their fertility. I was politically pro-choice. While I was in my residency, I had a change of heart. Now, this issue is so polarizing, so politicized, we really have to try to move beyond this. We have, from the pro-choice side, people like Merle Hoffman, a staunch defender of abortion rights, telling us how abortion is the most moral choice a woman can make. And the pro-life group 40 Days for Life is saying women deserve better than abortion and that abortion is the killing of a human life. We want to beat each other over the head with sound bites, and there's very little *actual conversation*. That's why I'm here: trying to create conversation."

Which he does for the next hour.

✝

Days later, he's still on the road, this time in Cromwell, Connecticut, in his room on the third floor of a Courtyard Marriot. His suitcase is open. His dress shirts are halfway out of the bag as if reluctant to be hung in the closet, so as not to get too comfortable in this room that is not home.

You can hear the traffic on Interstate-91, a perfect sound-track to an itinerant life. Through the window, you can see a line of fast food restaurants and chain stores — a homogenized landscape replicated throughout the country. In other words, this could be anywhere. And for a man who never imagined he'd be doing this much travel and this much talking, this feels like anywhere but home. He's tired. He misses his family. He misses his patients at his OB/GYN clinic in Virginia. He'll be heading home this afternoon.

But he's absolutely psyched (his word) about those conversations created at all those medical schools he's visited and all those bright-eyed future doctors to whom he's spoken.

"It's not speaking to the choir," he says. "The choir already is against abortion. They already know. What this is doing at the med schools is advancing the topic forward, decoupling it from politics."

In an hour, he'll be speaking to "the choir" — a couple dozen people from a right-to-life group in a convention room down on the first floor. It's an election year. They're wearing campaign pins in support of GOP candidates. They are gal-vanized in their opposition to President Barack Obama, an abortion-rights advocate who champions Planned Parenthood, the nation's largest abortion provider.

Their average age is probably about 65. Dr. Bruchalski will probably thank them for all their hard work and sacrifice over the years. He'll probably tell them he knows that he is standing on the shoulders of giants — they being the giants, they being the generation who refused to stand down when the right to abortion became the law of the land back in 1973, with the U.S. Supreme Court's Roe vs. Wade decision.

He'll certainly agree with them that abortion has been the greatest injustice, the greatest tragedy, to befall this nation. He'll probably tell them about the not-for-profit OB/GYN clinic he founded in 1994, financed largely through fundraising. Its founding principles are to practice excellent medicine, serve all women — many of them poor, many of them in crisis pregnancies — to see in them the face of Christ, and to follow the teachings of the Catholic Church with regards to biomedical ethics.

Similar to his talks to college medical students, there are things he will decidedly *not* mention, out of respect. He will not mention his belief regarding the future of abortion rights — that despite all the efforts of the pro-life movement, abortion will probably *always* remain legally available to women in the United States. He will not bring up the fact that despite efforts of the pro-life movement during the past 40 years, 1.3 million abortions are still performed each year. He will not mention he has friends who perform abortions — that without a one-on-one personal, civil, respectful relationship with the "opposition," few things will ever get accomplished. He will not mention it's unrealistic to believe that putting certain pro-life politicians into office can resolve the abortion issue, or that fighting it in the courts will change things. He won't say the only solution is changing hearts the way the Lord and His disciples did, through mercy. He will not mention what he believes is obvious — that, for the vast majority of Americans, the bishops no longer hold sway.

He won't mention these things because he only has about an hour and because he could pick any one of these sensitive topics and talk for two days about each. Also, he's helping to lead a new front in the pro-life movement, a different tack from this first generation's, and he's sensitive to the great risk that he might put his foot in his mouth.

He figures that once he's down in the convention room, as with the med students, he'll tailor his message to the crowd

— in the language of Christian morals and social outrage. Maybe he'll say something like this:

"In my profession of OB/GYN, they want you to push contraceptives on kids and hormones to older women. They want to put IUDs into teenagers. They want us to abort children. They want us to selectively reduce twins and triplets to get them to single babies because of the risks of in-vitro fertilization. We are truly in the slop."

He's said that before to pro-life crowds. He believes it just as much as he believes in the data he shares with med students.

Still, in his room, an hour before he's to take to the podium, he has just plopped down on the couch and breathed a heavy sigh.

"These are wonderful people," he says of the crowd he will speak to. "They come out here on a Saturday out of love for the cause and a determination to change things for the better. It's amazing."

He sounds a little discouraged. He made a promise to the Blessed Virgin Mary years ago in the midst of his conversion, and the promise was he would do everything within his power to help transform medicine so as to help transform the world. He's fairly certain the Courtyard Marriot is not where the battle needs to be waged. It's being waged in his clinic, one patient at a time, in med schools, and through relationships with people he disagrees with. That's become the key for him: Engage with people he disagrees with and whom disagree with him.

With the heart of St. Paul, he wishes to "become all things to all men" so that by all possible means he might save some (1 Cor 9:22). In that way, he's bilingual. He can speak to the converted and speak to med students in the same native tongue, with no contradictions, but just a slight tweak on emphasis.

Still, he's got the med students on his mind. He's got the Acts of the Apostles on his mind. He has concern that some in the pro-life movement have circled the wagons rather than going out into the world as the apostles did. He knows the only way to advance the cause is by understanding and engaging people through mercy and love and example.

He doesn't know what he's going to say yet to that crowd downstairs.

✝

Dr. Bruchalski was first drawn to accept the invitation to speak here in Cromwell because it is home of Holy Apostles Seminary, which always meant so much to his late mother who supported the institution.

"I came here to think of my mom," he says.

She and his father never minced words regarding the importance of a Catholic upbringing. They dedicated him to the Blessed Mother at a young age.

"I grew up in a great Polish family in New Jersey," Dr. Bruchalski says in an interview in his hotel room, "and every morning, we said a decade of the Rosary for the conversion of Russia. We asked for the intercession of many saints, and it just so happened that *Jezu, ufam Tobie!*, the Polish version of 'Jesus, I trust in You'— a phrase that Jesus begs us to repeat throughout our lives, particularly in times of distress — was a common phrase around our house."

As a boy, his family doctor was his role model because he was "simple, straightforward, and busy helping people get well," Dr. Bruchalski says. That's what Dr. Bruchalski wished to emulate. He wanted to help people, and to tie faith to action and action to faith. He had no clue how complicated that would become as of Monday, January 22, 1973. He was 12 years old at the time and shooting hoops in his driveway when his father arrived home from work with a heavy heart.

"Before he exited his VW Bug, he told me, 'Johnny, it's Black Monday. The Supreme Court legalized abortion, the killing of innocent babies. We will be punished.'"

Even when he grew into his teen years and became lukewarm in his faith, and even in college when he came to the conclusion his father had been wrong, Dr. Bruchalski would remember that day. It was his George Washington/cherry tree moment. That is to say, he knew he must not tell lies, particularly to himself.

"I simply bought the entire argument that humans would be better off economically and socially by controlling their fertility through chemicals, barriers, plastics, and surgery," he says. As he advanced in his schooling, he says, "I felt the Church had lost touch with regular people and was wrong on the point of women's issues and reproductive freedom." In med school, he would build intrauterine devices (IUDs) to prevent pregnancy, provide contraceptives, and learn sterilization. Then, when a professor suggested he could earn extra money by performing abortions, he began doing that, too.

"I would just do the procedure, and I didn't think much about it," he said. "At first, I was dealing with pregnancies that were early on — five or six weeks. But when I started to get into pregnancies that were further along, I'd see body parts, and it started to bother me. It bothered me greatly."

✝

Here's the first question Dr. Bruchalski raises with the med school students:

"Why is it that the number of Americans who identify themselves as pro-choice has been steadily declining? They're now the *minority*."

The polls bear that out. Gallup announced in May 2012 that only 41 percent of Americans now identified themselves as "pro-choice," down from 47 percent a year prior. Meanwhile, 50 percent now call themselves "pro-life." That's not to suggest all people who call themselves pro-life want abortion banned. But it does suggest Americans are increasingly questioning the morality of abortion and recognizing the humanity of the fetus.

One student at the University of Arizona raises her hand and suggests the reason for the trend could be the introduction of the Ultrasound that now allows the opportunity to view the fetus.

"I agree," Dr. Bruchalski says. "The fetus now becomes real to people. I believe that's the prime reason."

Here's the second question he poses, "Why is it that while 97 percent of family doctors report having encountered patients seeking abortion, only five to 15 percent will perform abortions?"

"It's a hassle," one male student says.

"Why is it a hassle?" Dr. Bruchalski asks.

"There's too much political and social stigma attached to it," the student responds.

"But *why* is there this stigma?" Dr. Bruchalski asks. "*Why* do many doctors who perform abortions feel professionally shunned? *Why* is that? Because they feel like they have to look over their shoulder in case some 'pro-life nut' decides to kill them? That's part of it, I'm sure. But that's not all of it."

And this is when he tries to make his case using an article published by the *Washington Post*, a publication no one could accuse of carrying water for the religious right-wing. The article is titled "A Hard Choice." The reporter follows a 24-year-old University of Maryland School of Medicine student who wants to go into the field of obstetrics and gynecology. The article begins at a lecture given by obstetrician and genetics expert Carol Meyers, who issues tough challenges to young medical students by asking, "How pro-choice are you?" Though she herself is pro-choice, nonetheless, Meyers feels it is irresponsible to teach abortion procedures without examining abortion's ethical dilemmas. Because the student being profiled in the piece, Leslie Wojick, is pro-choice, she feels her actions should support her words, so she volunteers to perform abortions. Yet she finds herself disgusted not just by the procedure but by the dehumanization of both the fetus and the mother. Leslie would not be dissuaded from her view that women have the right to have abortions, but she wanted nothing to do with it. She wanted to bring babies to term, not kill them.

"How pro-choice are you?" Dr. Bruchalski asks the students.

He doesn't *have* to mention the Blessed Mother. He doesn't *have* to mention Jesus Christ. All he needs to mention are statistics and data: the health risks of abortion; the increasing number of doctors who refuse to perform it; that the more we know about fetal development, the harder it becomes to dismiss the humanity of the fetus. Week three following conception: The fetus has a heart that beats with its own blood. Week five:

Eyes, legs, and hands are developing. Week six: The fetus has detectible brain waves, a mouth, and lips.

Those are facts, not religious beliefs.

"So what is the definition of personhood?" Dr. Bruchalski asks. "Is it still subjective?"

A young woman raises her hand and asks to what degree the roles of politics and social stigma played in his decision to stop performing abortions.

"For me," says Dr. Bruchalski, "it was the tactile experience. When you take a K-bar and you jam it up the cervix and it hits a rib, and you torque it into a woman's chest — when you take a cannula, the suction curette, and you enter the uterus and it hits the baby and the curette moves — it *moves*. That's what began to get to me. And then when they get bigger, you've got to dismember them. You have to place the parts on the table and count the limbs. It's brutal, visceral. It's difficult to watch, and it's difficult to do. You're eviscerating the fetus, and I felt it was eviscerating my humanity. As a physician, you've been sworn to protect life; something just doesn't jive.

"Then, many of the women I gave abortions to were not happy with it. Their boyfriends still broke up with them. In some instances, things got too casual. I was in a clinic, and a woman comes up to me and says, 'Thanks for the two-fer.' 'The two-fer?' I asked. She said, 'Yeah, I had twins, and you took out both of them.'

"It was coarse and casual. Things like this would start to bother me to the point where I said, 'I can't do this anymore.'"

What he doesn't explain to them is the other factor that caused him to stop performing abortions.

But he *will* explain it in his hotel room.

He says, "Christ and His Mother came a-callin.'"

✝

At first, he didn't listen to Christ's Mother, the Blessed Mother, when she spoke to his heart in 1987.

"I was studying medicine, and I was trying to discern about residency programs when a friend of mine invited me down to Mexico City. At the time, I was being a typical gynecologist. I believed that contraceptives would liberate women. When I visited the Basilica of Our Lady of Guadalupe, I very distinctly heard the words 'Why are you hurting me?' It was an internal voice. It was a woman's voice — very loving, very non-threatening. I thought the heat was getting to me. I tried to rationally explain it. But the voice was very clear. I didn't entirely understand it. But I believe that voice was Our Lady of Guadalupe trying to make me see what I was doing. But it would be years before I fully understood the message."

In the midst of his residency, 18 months in which he performed abortions, his mother took him on a pilgrimage to Medjugorje in Yugoslavia, where the Blessed Virgin Mary has reportedly been appearing and giving messages to bring people back to Christ. During quiet prayer time there, it became clear to Dr. Bruchalski that the Mother of God was repeating to him the words she used at the wedding feast in Cana (Jn 2:5) when she ordered the servants to obey her Son, "Do whatever He tells you."

What Jesus was telling Dr. Bruchalski to do was to practice medicine in a way that would maximize his faith. That meant, never to replace the patient with profit. Patients feel used and ignored rather than listened to. That meant never alienating himself from the reasons he went into medicine in the first place. Never allow care and compassion to become buried underneath technology and technical skills that have "turned the art and science of medicine into a mechanic's garage," he says. That meant understanding that while science and technology bring about amazing progress in medicine, "they don't bring redemption. The only person who brings redemption is Christ. So if you can't tie the two together, you're lost."

When he returned from Medjugorje, he eventually joined a pro-life practice in Maryland. But they didn't go far enough, he says. "They didn't serve the underserved. I said, 'There's got to be a better way to do this.'"

Together with his wife, Carolyn, and a few financial supporters, he took a leap of faith in 1994, starting the Tepeyac Family Center — first in his basement, and then growing into a full-fledged clinic in Arlington, Virginia. The clinic's namesake is the hill in Mexico where the Blessed Mother appeared to Juan Diego in 1531. Dr. Bruchalski says, "I put Tepeyac in the name to remind me why I was doing this. I need daily reminders."

The center delivers an average of 750 babies annually — 130 of which are to uninsured mothers. The center's 20-person staff handles upwards of 25,000 patient visits a year. Tepeyac does this at a time when medical reimbursements have decreased and malpractice premiums and overhead have increased.

"So far, we've remained financially solvent," he says. "People ask what's my five-year plan? The five-year plan is 'Jesus, I trust in You.'"

✝

He doesn't look so tired anymore up there in front of all those students in Phoenix. Clearly, he has their attention, and he's making the most of it.

"So with so few physicians willing to perform abortions," he says, "the American College of Obstetricians and Gynecologists knew they had a problem and had to do something different, so in an ethics-committee opinion in 2007, they decided to deny its members the right of conscience against abortion. In other words, despite your conscience or beliefs, you have to perform abortions or be complicit in them by finding a willing doctor for the patient."

While this policy has not become federally mandated, he has reason to fear it might be, Dr. Bruchalski says.

A student named Lolita raises her hand and asks, "But what are your thoughts about 'back-alley' abortions — that women will have abortions anyway, regardless of legality? Shouldn't physicians be trained to perform abortions just so it remains a safe procedure?"

He tells her that physicians already are, for all intents and purposes, trained to do the procedure since it isn't much different than performing a D&C, also known as dilation and curettage — a surgical procedure often performed after a first trimester miscarriage to stop bleeding.

"But legality isn't even the point," Dr. Bruchalski says. "The point I'm making is that people like me, we need a seat at the table. If I have a pro-life opinion, what the American College of Obstetricians and Gynecologists is saying is, 'Don't even bother going into OB/GYN.'"

"What about pregnancies due to rape or incest, or pregnant mothers already convicted of child abuse or on cocaine?" a male student asks. "We hear these heartbreaking stories. What do you do about that?"

"It's a hard question, I agree," Dr. Bruchalski says. He pauses for a moment.

"My approach is to always focus and take care of two patients — the mother and the child."

As much as he would like to finish that sentence with "… and then let the Holy Spirit take over from there," he knows he can't.

He tells the students that pro-life physicians and pro-choice physicians should seek to find "common ground."

"But how?" Lolita asks.

"If you believe abortion is a right," he says, "you need to do the procedure. And if you are pro-life, you need to go beyond serving 'just the fetus.' You should spend time working in pregnancy crisis centers. You should look at the mother in her family situation and go beyond 'saving the baby.'"

What he'd like to say, but doesn't, is "… and then let the Holy Spirit take over from there."

✝

"None of this is easy, man," Dr. Bruchalski, in his hotel room, says, with a sigh while reaching for his tie.

So here in this hotel room — no med students around, no pro-life activists around — what would he like to scream to the world through a bullhorn?

That's easy.

"The problems in healthcare today center around sinful behavior," he says. "We are aborting innocents. We are promoting dysfunctional families. We are encouraging young people to have sex outside of marriage. We are not serving the underserved. And we are gouging the people who can pay for healthcare. While Washington argues about policy, and while we have the red states and blue states, the Democrats and Republicans, the real issue, the real crisis, is that we're being seduced to move God's mercy out of healthcare. And the answer to the healthcare crisis is to bring God's mercy back into healthcare, and to do it in an integrated, organic way.

"You do it by practicing excellent medicine, by serving the underserved, and by following the teachings of the faith. Why? Because God's mercy is manifested in the 10 Commandments. In John 15, the Lord says our joy will be complete when we follow His Commandments. Don't put idols before Him. Don't put money before faith. Do not kill. It's God's mercy, through the Commandments and the teachings of the Church, that tells us who we are and how to live a life of joy and abundance. And what are we doing in healthcare? We are trying to move Christ out of it. That's why we need this message of the Divine Mercy. That's why living the Divine Mercy message and being an ambassador of Divine Mercy is so crucial."

He pauses. A car alarm is honking outside in the parking lot. He looks outside. People are stepping out from cars that have pro-life bumper stickers such as, "Abortion stops a beating heart."

Dr. Bruchalski jumps back onto his train of thought. "The thing is," he says, "young people are still going into medicine because they want to help people. They care about a person who is sick and who is poor. There is still that kernel of hope in their hearts — that desire to serve another in trouble. We have to give them opportunities to do so. In the end, I don't see any real help coming from the government or from a political solution, or from the medical profession. It will come from the ground up, from the grassroots."

He likens it to the message of Divine Mercy, considered "the greatest grassroots movement in the history of the Church" for its being laity-driven rather than clergy-driven. What attracts him to the message of Divine Mercy, as revealed through the *Diary of St. Faustina*, is the way Jesus stresses its importance for our well-being and our salvation, "Mankind will not have peace until it turns with trust to My mercy" (300).

"Look," says Dr. Bruchalski, "I've performed abortions. The reality is that Jesus can save any one of us. None of us are *too* far away. None of us are *too* lost. Yes, Jesus' mercy affected me. He doesn't look back on my past. I have been forgiven."

Knowing that just makes it easier for him to befriend colleagues who perform abortions, one of which, a doctor from Florida, is in the midst of a conversion.

"He's a friend of mine, even though he is murdering babies. You have to become friends with them. You have to form relationships. We talk about being in a 'culture war.' I phrase it as, 'We're fighting principalities and powers. The enemy is sin and Satan.' So for me, the enemy is not 'the other.' It's ourselves. It's our own weaknesses. It's our own lack of conversations with our family and friends. It's our denial that we, too, need the Lord to turn us from hearts of stone to hearts of flesh. We have to love and not judge till the point where our enemies say, 'I want your peace, and I don't know how to get it. I want what you have, and I don't know how to get it.' And all the while we need to keep saying to ourselves, 'Jesus, I trust in You.' Why? In order to believe it."

In 2000, Dr. Bruchalski founded Divine Mercy Care, a not-for-profit organization whose motto is "to transform hearts through healthcare." It serves as the fundraising arm of Tepeyac Family Center. About 40 percent of his patients are Catholic, 40 percent evangelical, and the remaining are agnostic, Jewish, and Muslim.

"What we do is we try to encourage people, if they are not praying or meditating, they need to do that, to get them in touch with that higher power," he says. "You can't slam them over the head and talk to them in a language they don't understand. Over time, God does the hard work. We bring it up, saying, 'We'll pray for you.' Everybody appreciates that.

"Many of the people in our practice have been on the other side of the fence before. We've used contraceptives. We've done abortions. And so we don't throw stones at anyone. In fact, it's God's mercy that brings people around. We grab their hand and say, 'Let's just say a little prayer before we go a little further.'"

He's in the elevator now heading down to deliver his talk. "None of this is easy, man," he says again.

But he thinks he knows what to talk about to the crowd. He will thank them for their work and tell them about his college tour and about Divine Mercy Care.

"I think this is what they need to hear about. They need hope," he said. "I need to give them hope."

He cinches his tie.

"You know, I believe there's going to be a second Pentecost," he says. "I believe we're *living* in it right now, and I mean this from a very practical, grassroots level. Divine Mercy is the vehicle for the new birth because it's the great equalizer: We're all sinners. We all need mercy. And when we receive mercy from others and from God, it changes *everything* — everything. This is practical stuff, not 'religious fanaticism.'"

The elevator dings, and the doors open to the first floor.

"I'm in OB/GYN," he says. "I see everything as a new birth."

Felix Carroll

CHAPTER 9

Bryan Thatcher

'All I Had to Do Was Ask'

... God usually chooses the weakest and simplest souls as tools for His greatest works.

— Diary of St Faustina, 464

Southwest Airlines Flight 2695 from Tampa, Florida, touches down in Albuquerque, New Mexico, just before 7 p.m. From out of the plane steps Dr. Bryan Thatcher, Annie Karto, and Bryan's son Christopher. The three meet up in the terminal with Lee Bowers, who just flew in from Texas.

Soon, they all have their luggage — suitcases filled with clothes, of course, but also with Divine Mercy materials, song lyrics, and written testimonies of how Christ has transformed their lives. The next day — Saturday, August 11, 2012 — will be a big day. Bryan, Annie, and Lee have come to New Mexico to help convert hearts — to share with parishioners in the rural town of Moriarty what they know for certain about God's greatest attribute, mercy.

People will travel from as far as 60 miles. People like Ethel Trujillo and Anna Marie Villegas, who will emerge from the program feeling spiritually renewed. Like a woman named Bonnie who had an abortion 30 years ago and who will cry with joy listening to the testimonies, as she finally realizes Jesus loves her and forgives her. Like Marlys Keenan, a local newspaper reporter who has nine stories due the following evening. But still, she'll come.

Why?

Because about three years ago, Marlys was, in her own words, "starving to death, spiritually." Then, she started reading the *Diary of St. Faustina*, and she couldn't put it down.

Many of the 100 people who will come for the daylong program, called a "Day of Reflection," picked up the *Diary* at one point in their lives, too. Its reading led to reevaluations of everything — their lives, the Lord, their crosses, their obligations. For hearts that are broken, for lives that seem in ruins, for souls who yearn to know God and who seek closeness with Him, the *Diary* tends to have that effect. They'll come to delve deeper into the message of Divine Mercy, a message that calls us to approach God in prayer, repenting for our sins, and asking for His mercy. It's a call to be merciful to others, to extend love and forgiveness to others just as He does to us. Most of all, it's a call to completely trust in Jesus.

Bryan, Annie, and Lee — members of Eucharistic Apostles of The Divine Mercy (EADM), based outside of Tampa — have put on these programs for more than 14 years in parishes throughout the United States. Still, 14 years down the road, and the wattage never dims. Sunday morning, 14 hours after the event in Moriarty concludes, they'll all feel strangely the same: exhausted, like they just ran a marathon, but exhilarated, like they want to run another one. Bryan will get up in his hotel room in Moriarty. He'll pack his bags for his return trip home to Tampa. He'll shake his head in wonder.

"That was a powerful day," he'll say, folding a pair of socks as the sun peeks through the blinds. "What a job I have — I travel and meet these wonderful people who are trying to lead good lives. We help inspire them. But the thing is, they help to inspire us, too. It's an amazing thing."

✝

Some people seem to be born with an unwavering faith. Others get there the hard way, often after they've hit rock bottom. Bryan Thatcher doesn't recommend the rock-bottom path toward faith, but it's the one he knows. It's the only path most people he meets know — like people in Moriarty, or the thousands of people around the world to whom he's had the privilege to minister. Only through suffering could he see the face of Jesus and realize he is nothing without Him.

He was handed the *Diary of St. Faustina* in 1992. It was the right book at the right time. Ever self-effacing, Bryan says, "I was down so low, I could play hand ball off the side of the curb." He describes himself at the time as among the most "broken of the broken."

Paradoxically, at the time, Bryan was treating the sickest of the sick. A doctor with a specialty in gastro-intestinal medicine, he was making a lot of money, he was helping a lot of people, and he was highly regarded in his field and in his community. He had it all, so it seemed — a successful life, large house, nice car, and a loving family. On the flip side, he saw a lot of death. He was burning out. He was spending nearly every waking hour in intensive care units and emergency rooms caring for his patients. He was rarely home. And, eventually, he was unfaithful to his wife.

He was a mess, and it all finally hit home in 1991, during a medical conference in Mexico City. When he had an afternoon off, he decided to visit that city's most famous landmark, the Basilica of Our Lady of Guadalupe where he promptly broke down in tears amidst thousands of people in the street. It wasn't the Basilica or the statues or the Blessed Sacrament that moved him to tears. It was the people. It was their way of life. Just look at them. Most were obviously poor. Yet, there they were smiling, absolutely joyful. They ate simple food from street vendors. Pistachios, pineapple, quesadillas. They wore simple clothes. They held the hands of their loved ones. They swung their children in their arms. Bryan felt like a fool. "Look at all that love," he thought to himself. "Guileless love. And what have I done?" He had complicated his life at the expense of his family and his soul. Yeah, he was helping people. But he was dying inside all the while. "Here I am, this rich gringo amidst all these poor people, and I was the one all messed up," Bryan says.

"I thought, 'Am I *really* happy?'" The answer then was: Of course, not. "I felt trapped but didn't know how to get 'un-trapped.' I was the one who was poor — poor in spirit. I was a 'high society, successful physician.'" But how successful was he if his marriage was falling apart? If he rarely saw his children? If he rarely practiced his faith?

When he returned home, things got worse because his attempts to change were short lived. He fell back into the same patterns and same sins until the day a friend handed him a copy of the *Diary*. Bryan took it home and started reading it. A quote jumped out at him, a quote that wound up changing his life, changing his career, changing everything. It's the passage in entry 723 where Jesus tells St. Faustina, "The greater the sinner, the greater the right he has to My mercy."

"I began to read the *Diary*, and I began to feel hope," Bryan says. He begged God to forgive him for all the ways he had messed things up. God, in turn, showed him in powerful ways that He was listening and that He loved him. One pivotal moment occurred soon after Bryan started reading the *Diary*. After Mass one morning, a man Bryan didn't know approached him and told him that he felt God wanted him to speak with Bryan. Bryan thought, "*Uh-oh, what am I in for?*" They decided to have breakfast together. After they sat down, the man began telling Bryan how he had recently gotten a divorce and how he had marital affairs. Bryan again thought, "*Oh, boy, what's this all about.*"

But it turns out the two men hit it off. They had a lot in common and a lot to talk about. They started to meet and pray with one another. That man, too, had been inspired to draw closer to God through the *Diary of St. Faustina*. Others began joining them. Together, they turned to Scripture, the *Catechism of the Catholic Church*, and the *Diary*. They were from all walks of life. They shared a common goal: to turn from sin and straighten their lives out through devotion to Jesus, the Divine Mercy.

Spiritually, Bryan's life was being transformed. That transformation led him to reevaluate his career and his role as husband and father. "I remember on one occasion in particular, I was trying to discern if God wanted me to spread His Divine Mercy," recalls Bryan. "I felt that I was not capable of doing that because of my sinfulness. So I asked God for a sign. I was really in a quandary because I didn't feel worthy or capable. How could I evangelize, one so broken? I opened the *Diary*, randomly, and landed on entry 464."

In that entry, St. Faustina writes:

> During a meditation on humility, an old doubt returned: that a soul as miserable as mine could not carry out the task which the Lord was demanding [of me]. Just as I was analyzing this doubt, the priest who was conducting the retreat interrupted his train of thought and spoke about the very thing that I was having doubts about; namely, that God usually chooses the weakest and simplest souls as tools for His greatest works; that we can see that this is an

undeniable truth when we look at the men that He chose to be His apostles; or again, when we look at the history of the Church and see what great works were done by souls that were the least capable of accomplishing them; for it is just in this way that God's works are revealed for what they are, the works of God. When my doubts had completely disappeared, the priest resumed his conference on humility.

It was then that Bryan was reminded of the story of the Prodigal Son, and how the Father was waiting with open arms to welcome the son home. God was welcoming Bryan home.

"I started to feel the intense presence of God helping me to understand that I am somebody," Bryan says, "not because of my educational achievements, position on the job, my income, or the type of car I drove, but because I was created in the image and likeness of God. And I began to realize in a deeper way that God loves *me*. And He is a merciful God, ready to forgive. All I had to do was ask."

From that breakfast encounter after Mass sprang a world-wide ministry, Eucharistic Apostles of The Divine Mercy (EADM). Instead of treating people's physical sufferings, Bryan treats their spiritual sufferings. With EADM, he promotes Divine Mercy through prayer cenacles, works of mercy, Eucharistic adoration, and praying the Chaplet of the Divine Mercy for the sick and dying. EADM is a lay outreach of the Marian Fathers of the Immaculate Conception. EADM, which now has more than 3,000 cenacles, received a papal blessing from Blessed John Paul II in 2003.

†

"I feel that people need to hear the message out here," says Barbara Christian. It was her idea to bring the Day of Reflection to Moriarty, New Mexico. "What I'm hoping is that people from different parishes are inspired by this and that they take the message of Divine Mercy back to their parishes and breathe new life into them."

Barbara, who lives in Moriarty, has a gift for breathing life into things. Literally. She's a paramedic in Albuquerque. It could be people dying in an alleyway. It could be the beautiful garden that she planted and tends on the grounds here at Our Lady of Mount Carmel Church in Moriarty. It could be for her fellow parishioners themselves, to whom, with the cooperation of her pastor, Fr. William Young, she has recently introduced the Divine Mercy devotions.

Barbara and her husband, Tom, meet Bryan and the others at the airport. They greet each other with hugs. They share a dinner together before Barbara and Tom drop Bryan, Annie, Lee, and Christopher off at the hotel for the evening. By 8:30 on Saturday morning, everything is set at Our Lady of Mount Carmel. The program will begin in a half hour. Bag lunches have been prepared. Homemade signs are hung on the walls. One quotes the Chaplet of the Divine Mercy, "*For the sake of His sorrowful Passion, have mercy on us and on the whole world.*"

It's already hot outside. Industrial-sized fans whirr in the parish hall, where the attendees start the morning with coffee and muffins that are arranged around a foot-tall statue of Jesus.

Our Lady of Mount Carmel is located out at the edge of Moriarty, a town that straddles the famous old Route 66. Desert sage and simple, low-slung houses with corrugated steel roofs disappear off into the vanishing point, off where the land meets the sky, which seems impossibly big and impossibly blue. The church itself looks like something you'd see on an old and faded New Mexico postcard — beautiful in its simplicity, sheathed in desert beige stucco, with a tiny, maroon-colored bell tower that seems slightly tilted as if its bell has been struck with more muscle, more zeal, than was originally intended.

Through pockets of Divine Mercy devotees in the four churches that comprise Estancia Valley Catholic Parish, the message of Divine Mercy has been ringing across these high desert plains for several years now. Bryan Thatcher — though he would absolutely hate for someone to tell him this — is a celebrity in parishes like this. People have seen him on the Eternal World Television Network (EWTN). They've read about him in Catholic magazines and have read his books. His ministry has inspired people like Jim and Betty Summer, from nearby Estancia, who enter the hall just after 8:30 a.m.

"Divine Mercy is big with my wife and me," explains Jim. So much so, that the two have embarked on a rather large work of mercy — founding a safe house for victims of domestic violence. "My wife lost a sister to domestic violence in 1982," says Jim, who works as a bail bondsman, "and it has always laid heavy on her heart to do something about it."

Judith Costello also enters. She talks of how Our Lady of Mount Carmel began the daily 3 o'clock hour devotion of praying the Chaplet of the Divine Mercy. "It's a small group," she says, "but we're hoping it will grow as a result of this event today."

Father Young also walks in, giving a wave to the room. He, himself, has had a devotion to the Divine Mercy for years. Later in the day, he'll tell the attendees how the *Diary* provides "a deep and rich means by which we may grow in our spiritual lives."

"Here, we have a nun, St. Faustina, who has much to write certainly about convent life, but her words are directly, in a sense, translatable into our lives as well, whether we're single people, divorced, married, parents, grandparents," he'll say. He'll also ask everyone to pray for people "who do not, or will not, pray for mercy and forgiveness. Pray for people who do not think that God ever could, or would, forgive them."

At 9 a.m., everyone files into the chapel where Annie has begun singing, *"Holy, holy, holy is His name."*

Father Young brings in a first-class relic of St. Faustina. When the music stops, he thanks Bryan, Annie, and Lee for coming (and Christopher, too, now one of seven children of Bryan and his wife, Susan). Father Young also thanks God for the message of Divine Mercy, "this beautiful expression He gives us through St. Faustina of His powerful divine love." And he prays for God's help that all present "remain faithful to the gift of our Catholic faith."

So, the Day of Reflection begins.

"We come from far away, but we're united in a greater understanding of the mercy of God," says Bryan. "We come here as fellow Catholics and sinners learning to trust in God and trying to walk the walk."

Yep, it's one thing to say "Jesus, I trust in You." It's another to actually do so, particularly in times of crisis, as Bryan has come to find out.

†

By 1996, he had left his medical career to spread the message of Divine Mercy full-time.

One morning in early November 1996, Bryan was exhausted having just returned from a conference in Denver where he gave a talk. He stepped onto his back patio, opened the gate to the family's swimming pool, and walked out to the backyard. When his oldest son, Bryan, called for him to come to the front yard to help start the lawn mower, Bryan unknowingly left the pool gate open. The gate remained open as he drove his oldest daughter, Andrea, to swim practice.

Fifteen minutes into leaving the house, he received a frantic call on his cell phone from his son Bryan who said 15-month-old John Paul, was dead. The pool gate had been left open. Bryan's wife, Susan, found John Paul floating face down. He had no pulse. He was blue. Bryan told his son to call 911 and have Susan start CPR, as he and Andrea rushed back home.

"During the drive home, I began praying with all my heart and asking Jesus to have mercy on John Paul and me," Bryan says. "Realizing that I had been distracted and had left the pool gate open, I was overwhelmed by guilt. I envisioned my little boy as he struggled for air. What really hurt the most was that John Paul had brought such healing and joy to our marriage and family. He had been a big part of that healing process and new direction in life — a child of promise for my wife and me."

"*Jesus, why would You take John Paul from us now?*" Bryan's heart cried out.

"Then, as I prayed in the car to Jesus, Our Lady, and all the saints, I realized that at this moment, I needed to trust in Jesus on a deeper level," Bryan says. "I had just told hundreds of people at a conference in Denver about Divine Mercy and the need for trust. Now, I was rushing to my own home back in Florida, needing to trust like never before.

"As Andrea and I came to a major intersection, we were stopped by a red light. The Scripture passage of Abraham being asked to sacrifice Isaac, the child of the promise (see Gen 22), came to mind. I told God I didn't understand why He would take John Paul from us at this time. Still, I offered my son back to Him. I also thanked God for the time He had given us with John Paul. I told Jesus that I placed my trust in Him and wanted only that His will be done. I felt a deep sense of peace after that. Yet I drove home all the faster to see what I would find."

By the time he got home, the paramedics were loading John Paul into the ambulance while performing CPR. John Paul was bloated and unresponsive, but he had a pulse now — weak though it was.

"Upon arriving at the hospital, I called my sister and told her to pray for John Paul that night at her prayer group," recalls Bryan.

John Paul's condition improved day by day. Within two days, he was released — a healthy baby boy.

"I saw my sister a couple of weeks later," says Bryan. "She said to me, 'The morning following our prayer group, my friend Irma called and said that she knew John Paul was going to recover. While praying in the morning, she had received a vision of Abraham offering Isaac back to God the Father. Then Jesus, the Divine Mercy, stepped in the middle and gave him back.' Tears streamed down my cheeks, and I said to her, 'Well, let me tell you the rest of the story.'"

The rest of the story is that Bryan has never been the same since that lesson in trusting Jesus.

†

"How can we love the God we cannot see if we cannot love the brothers and sisters we can see?" Bryan asks the crowd in Moriarty. He's urging attendees to be Christlike in their daily lives. Forgiveness, he says, "opens the door to receiving God's mercy. Through Divine Mercy — lived in the home and in the workplace — mankind can begin to solve the greatest problems it faces today. We need to pray that God changes our hearts. We need to let our hearts be turned into hearts of flesh, of love, of caring. That will change the family and people at work, and we'll begin to see healing. Through Divine Mercy, we truly will transform the world."

At one point in her *Diary*, St. Faustina records how Christ once commanded her, "Tell aching mankind to snuggle close to My merciful Heart, and I will fill it with peace" (1074). Lee quotes that passage in her talk, a talk that gives the basics of the Divine Mercy message and devotion and its historical context. Then, Lee quotes from the *Diary*, where Jesus says, "I do not want to punish aching mankind, but I desire to heal it, pressing it to My Merciful Heart" (1588).

Annie, whose musical CDs feature songs that promote Eucharistic Adoration, the Sacraments, Mary, religious vocations, and respect for the sanctity of life, tells attendees how she came to dedicate her life to spreading Divine Mercy. She left home at 17 to marry her high school sweetheart. With much heartache, six years later she found herself divorced with two small boys.

"In haste, I remarried outside the Church," Annie says, "In 1989, my mother invited me to her home in the Ozark Mountains. At that time, my present marriage was in serious trouble, and I felt like a failure in so many areas in my life. I remember sitting in the chapel in front of Jesus exposed in the monstrance. A storm had rolled in, and thunder was echoing off the mountains. I could not take my eyes off of Jesus in the monstrance. I realized with a new awareness that He could see every sin and defect in my character, and I felt ashamed and broken. But, instead of feeling condemned, I felt a river of mercy flood my soul, as if washing it clean. I experienced such a tender love and forgiveness for all my sins and poor choices.

"The next day, I knew I must go to confession," Annie continues, "and as I walked in, I noticed the Divine Mercy image on the wall. The priest, a family friend, looked at me with tenderness. I remember him saying, 'How many people do you think are out there like you, Annie? God's people who are broken, sinful, in need of healing?'"

He then encouraged her to spread the message of Divine Mercy the rest of her life. Great miracles of healing have followed. She was able to have her marriage blessed in the Church.

Annie concludes with words of St. Faustina, who wrote, "The mercy of the Lord I will sing forever. Before all the people will I sing it. For it is God's greatest attribute and for us an unending miracle" (*Diary*, 522).

Meanwhile, Marlys, the reporter, is one of several in the audience with tears in their eyes. While listening to the talks, she's thinking of her son who was killed in a car accident in January. She explains later that he suffered many years from drug addiction and sin. But two years ago, he showed up at midnight Mass. She remembers. She saw him coming down the center aisle.

"He's with me today," Marlys says. "I can feel his presence. And I know that because of St. Faustina, Christ granted my son mercy at the hour of his death. I know everything is OK."

Despite having so many newspaper stories to write by tomorrow evening, Marlys isn't worried. She's here because, among the other things, she knows for certain, "Every minute I give to God, He gives back to me, and more," she says.

Bonnie is among the others crying tears of joy. Annie, as she was singing, noticed Bonnie. "Just seeing her face inspired me as I was up there singing," Annie later says. Bonnie had an abortion 30 years ago. And even though she confessed her sin, she was unable to experience the forgiveness she had received. Instead, she continued to struggle with feelings of guilt and shame.

"But here, today, for the first time," she says, "I experienced the forgiveness that I've never experienced before. I had a burden lifted from my shoulders today. I can go forward now."

Bryan has given such programs to audiences with as many as 2,000 people and as few as five people.

"It doesn't matter," he says. "I'll go anywhere because I know that when a person encounters the message of Divine Mercy it changes a life, and it has a ripple effect that's extraordinary. This is what happened in my life."

The Day of Reflection in Moriarty ends with Holy Mass. Afterwards, Barbara and her husband, Tom, bring Bryan, Annie, Lee, and Christopher back to their house for a lasagna dinner. Father Young joins them. They say grace, afer which there's a brief silence. Barbara folds her hands together and says with a beaming smile, "It was a beautiful day."

"Another beautiful day," says Bryan. "God is amazing."

Felix Carroll

CHAPTER 10

*Stan Brody

Forgiveness Is the Code of the Road

"Stan Brody" and "Gina" requested their real names
not to be used in order to protect their privacy.

Jesus to St. Faustina:

Souls that make an appeal to My mercy delight Me. To such Souls I grant even more graces than they ask.

— Diary of St. Faustina, 1146

As a boy, he would look up from the front steps of his modest home in Chattanooga, Tennessee, and marvel at the big homes that command attention along the towering ridgeline of Lookout Mountain.

"Wow, those people must be rich," Stan Brody would think to himself.

Someday. Maybe someday, it'll be me.

Someday came. A big house, new cars, vacations in Acapulco and Hawaii. He "made the dollar holler," as he puts it. Then, progressively, his marriage crumbled. One morning, in 2007, he packed up his clothes, muscled his recliner onto the bed of his pick-up, and drove away.

Now, he's 47 years old, and the year is 2012. Driving along the Tennessee River in an end-run around Lookout Mountain, Stan doesn't think much about towering views and big houses anymore. He's on Interstate 24 heading west on a six-hour drive across Tennessee to Memphis, a trip he does almost weekly upon the close of another work week.

If Stan's life now speaks volumes to the power of Divine Mercy, then Chattanooga and Memphis represent its two bookends. Chattanooga is where he puts his old life of materialism, unrepentant sin, and selfishness behind him. Memphis is where his nascent life of contrition, salvation, and self-sacrifice has begun.

"I really thought my whole adult life that I was a good man, doing everything right," says Stan. He's got the build of a fullback, and his Southern enunciation casually dispenses surplus syllables. "Mirror" is "meer." "Over here" is "aheere."

He's shouldering the wheel. It's the dead of winter. Up ahead, icicles hang from along the northern escarpment of Monteagle Mountain. This stretch of interstate is often referenced as one of the nation's most treacherous. The road signs warn of the potential of boulders coming loose and tumbling upon the highway.

What if God struck him down right now, at this very moment? Is he prepared to meet his Maker? He thinks about these things now. He never used to.

In his old life, Stan didn't see the warning signs that his soul might be in peril till he found himself face to face with the father of a young woman with whom he was having an affair. Stan fathered two children with the young woman, all the while keeping the home fires burning back in Chattanooga. That woman's father could have picked up a shotgun and dealt with Stan the old-fashioned way. Instead, he picked up the *Diary of St. Faustina* and sought to save Stan's soul.

Motoring along the interstate, Stan points to the sign for Browns Ferry Road.

"There's a lot of Civil War history here," he says.

The Union Army pried open a supply route here in 1863, a pivotal campaign that eventually upended the Confederate Army's grip on Appalachia. Who knows, maybe we could have ended up with a fractured confederacy in the South to this day. There are layers upon layers of history around these parts, including that of the fractured Brody family. Stan points across the Tennessee River to Moccasin Bend Mental Health Institute off to the right. Both his parents spent time there during his childhood. Both struggled with substance abuse. His parents spent decades ensnared in nasty legal suits with each other. His father once told Stan that if his mother's hair ever caught fire, he wouldn't even waste his own spit to put the fire out.

His parents divorced when Stan was five years old. Stan was the youngest of two. His brother was born brain damaged, unable to hear and speak. Growing up, their father showed little interest in his kids. Stan played baseball through high school. His father never attended a single game.

In contrast, his mother was smitten with her two boys. She would drag them to rollicking Baptist religious revivals. "Faith," says Stan, "was burned into my roots, into my soul."

But his faith came with qualifications — ones that undercut his pursuit of holiness. Namely, when he saw the world around him — the less-than-saintly lives of Christians, the ones who went to church on Sundays and to the taverns on Mondays, who sang hymns one moment and swore the next — he found a perfect excuse to turn tail and run from organized religion.

The home on high would be something with a roof over it. Maybe it would have an inground swimming pool, too. Heaven would resemble something along the lines of those homes on Lookout Mountain.

By 2005, he had a wife and three teenage sons. Stan had become a sunglasses tycoon, having opened small retail stores in malls throughout the southeastern United States. He made lots of money. He built a 5,000-square-foot home on four acres. His boys always had everything they wanted — nice clothes, video games, sports equipment, you name it. He bought new cars whenever he wanted. The house was filled with expensive antiques and state-of-the-art electronics.

"Whatever I wanted to do, I did," Stan says.

That included cheating on his wife.

He met Gina, a fallen-away Catholic, in 2003 during his business travels. She was nearly half his age. "*Whoa, she resembles Jennifer Garner*," he thought to himself, referring to the actress. She was working as a sales clerk in his Memphis sunglasses shop. She became pregnant by him and had a girl she named Paige. A year later, she became pregnant by him again and gave birth to James. To cover his tracks, he told lie upon lie upon lie until he would lose track of the original lie.

Still, this affair and these children had no noticeable affect on Stan's life back in Chattanooga. He led two lives. Moreover, though he and his wife shared the same roof, they had already grown apart. The romance was over. With three high-spirited boys and one hot-headed husband, she simply had too much testosterone under one roof as it was. Still, making $8,000 a month, Stan provided for his family in Chattanooga. He loved his sons in Chattanooga dearly. He was a good father to them. Or so he thought.

"I was really a pig-headed idiot," Stan says, behind the wheel.

We're crossing into the Central Time Zone by Nashville. The clock falls back an hour. It's 3:52 p.m. Then — *poof!* — it's back to 2:52 p.m. Just imagine if you could wave a wand, then — *poof!* — you could go back in time to a moment of your choosing. Stan would give anything to have a "do-over" — to set his watch back to those days when his children were small, a boisterous clutch of impressionable boyhood craning their necks up at him, hanging on his every word.

There's no doubt about what tops the list of things he would change.

"If I could go back 20 years and let my three boys see their dad live his life the way their dad lives his life now —" His voice trails off.

His boys are now 25-, 22-, and 19-year-olds. Stan remains very close to them. Recently, he sat them down. This is what he said: "I was there for you, but I wasn't there for you the way you needed to see me there. I gave you all these things, but you never saw me on my knees praying to our Lord and Savior, Jesus Christ. It was my responsibility to make sure you get to heaven. If you had seen me as a man of faith, maybe some of the trials and tribulations in your lives would have been different. But it's not too late. It's never too late."

He says to me, "I know they can see me now living my faith. I just wish they could have seen it when they were children, small children. We need to lead by example. That's my main goal, to make sure those boys go to heaven. I still owe them so much. I've let them down. It's on me."

Stan's ex-wife has since remarried. She and Stan maintain a good relationship.

The land gets flat. You can see the Nashville skyline off to the right. Stan has driven from the Eastern Time Zone into the Central Time Zone, chasing a setting sun toward a woman he loves and the two young children they have together.

His cell phone rings. It's Gina.

"*Hi, Honey,*" he says. " *... Clear and sunny in Memphis? ... 67 degrees? Nice, nice. ... Are you getting the kids? ... Be careful. ... OK, I love you.*"

Gina and Stan are engaged to be married — in the Church. What a long, strange, blessed trip it's been, thanks to the Merciful Lord and a man named Jay Hastings.

✝

The dining table and chairs have long since been consigned to storage in the home of Jay Hastings and his wife, Patte, just outside of Memphis. In their place is a veritable bunker of folders, Divine Mercy materials, printed prayer requests, and a copy of the *Diary of St. Faustina* that looks on the verge of being loved right out of its binding.

"I'm always referring to it," says Jay, the founder of the worldwide ministry, Society of St. Faustina of The Divine Mercy. "I started highlighting the passages that seemed most important and wound up highlighting almost all the *Diary*, and when I didn't have a highlighter, I dog-eared the corner of the page."

The Society consists of Divine Mercy apostles who ensure that the Chaplet of the Divine Mercy is being prayed during every hour of the day. More than 1,300 people in 33 countries have joined up and committed to praying during an hour each day for three things: the promotion of the Divine Mercy devotion; the sick and dying in the hour that you pray; and people about to commit mortal sin.

Jay sits down at his computer. To give a glimpse of the vastness of his volunteer ministry, he opens his e-mail, and the inbox becomes engulfed by a rising tide of new prayer requests — for a five-year-old boy with a brain tumor fighting for his life; for a financial miracle; for a high school student to pass all his classes; for a father who has prostate cancer and a friend who has breast cancer; for a full conversion to Catholicism of a beloved friend; for the complete healing from leukemia of a nine-year-old girl; and on and on.

A night owl as well as an early bird, Jay tends to each e-mail, gathering each prayer intention, responding to the e-mailers with fitting passages from the *Diary* and recommending they obtain an image of the Divine Mercy, which the Lord said was a vessel of grace.

"We see miraculous things," Jay says, "because we believe in the power of the chaplet."

Back in 2002, when Jay and Patte lived unassuming lives free of prayer requests from Panama, or Zambia, or Burma, or you name it — when their dining room was still a dining room — Jay felt compelled to make a prayerful commitment to trust God more and to devote more of his life to Him. "When I opened that door, He sent me St. Faustina," says Jay, a 56-year-old father of four who sells insurance for a living. He soon discovered the *Diary of St. Faustina.* Through the *Diary,* he says, "I was able to understand the role we can all play as dispensers of God's mercy."

At a time when he was just learning about Divine Mercy, his parish, St. Ann's, was lent a relic of St. Faustina. Saint Ann's pastor, Fr. Bruce Cinquegrani, put Jay in charge of organizing a Divine Mercy novena leading up to the feast of Christ the King. During the novena the whole diocese was invited to venerate the relic. The novena proved a great success and led many parishioners to become devoted to the Divine Mercy message.

Jay's devotion soon took an unexpected turn. One day, during Holy Communion, he says he underwent a life-changing experience. "When I received the Host, it broke in half on my tongue, which had never happened to me before," he recalls. "In my heart, I heard the words, 'Help Me repair the Body of Christ.' Identifying the phrase with the broken Host, I was deeply moved."

Jay then received the inspiration to get people to pray the Chaplet of the Divine Mercy every hour of the day, and thus, "to help repair the Body of Christ spiritually and through our individual acts of mercy," he explains. As recorded in St. Faustina's *Diary,* Jesus attaches extraordinary promises to the recitation of the chaplet. At one point, Jesus transports St. Faustina and places her in front of a man who is dying and who has demons attacking his soul. Saint Faustina continuously prays the chaplet before him, and soon the demons disappear as mercy engulfs the man's soul (see *Diary,* 1565).

Through St. Faustina, Jesus speaks in the *Diary* of the power of the chaplet. "Whoever will recite it will receive great mercy at the hour of death" (687). "When they say this chaplet in the presence of the dying, I will stand between My Father and the dying person, not as the just Judge but as the Merciful Savior" (1541). "It takes about seven minutes to pray the chaplet," says Jay. "God makes things so simple for us."

If there's one single *Diary* passage that serves as the mission statement for the Society, it's passage 1074. "We want to approach the Lord with trust," says Jay, paraphrasing the passage. "Jesus told St. Faustina that when we approach Him with trust, we will be filled with such an abundance of graces that we will not be able to contain the graces within ourselves, so we will radiate them to other souls."

That trust has amounted to countless spiritual dividends. Stan and Gina, not least of all.

Christianity is often described as the easiest religion to explain but the hardest to live. We are to love God above all things. We are to love our neighbors as ourselves. We are to unite ourselves to God's Heart through prayer and works of mercy. We are to accept God's will with thankfulness and humility. Jay can recite chapter and verse of the Gospels and the *Diary* about our call as Christians.

But then his daughter, whom he raised as a Catholic, got pregnant by a married man. Then, she got pregnant again by the same married man. Who was this guy? Stan was practically a no-show in Memphis. Jay and Patte didn't even meet him after the birth of James. By then, Jay and Patte had become the primary caregivers to their two young grandchildren.

Jay would like to say he and Patte welcomed Stan into their home with open arms, but he cannot. The actions of Stan and Gina wounded them to the point of near emotional paralysis. But you have to not only proclaim your faith, you must also live it. Jay knew this. Mercy is what Christ demands from us. Intellectually, Jay understood this. But this understanding needed to travel from his head to his heart.

He kept returning to one particular *Diary* passage from entry 1549 where St. Faustina writes:

I want to live in the spirit of faith. I accept everything that comes my way as given me by the loving will of God, who sincerely desires my happiness. And so I will accept with submission and gratitude everything that God sends me. I will pay no attention to the voice of nature and to the promptings of self-love. Before each important action, I will stop to consider for a moment what relationship it has to eternal life and what may be the main reason for my undertaking it: is it for the glory of God, or for the good of my own soul, or for the good of the souls of others? If my heart says yes, then I will not swerve from carrying out the given action, unmindful of either obstacles or sacrifices. I will not be frightened into abandoning my intention. It is enough for me to know that it is pleasing to God. On the other hand, if I learn that the action has nothing in common with what I have just mentioned, I will try to elevate it to a loftier sphere by means of a good intention. And if I learn that something flows from my self-love, I will cancel it out right from the start.

"The actions of Stan and Gina were irresponsible and immature, and we were left dealing with the consequences," Jay says. "But we learned and we struggled and finally responded to the situation the way Jesus wants us to respond. We are not to respond to sin with anger and animosity and retribution. Our only response can be to love. Love is the only thing that heals."

Stan soon declared he wanted to be a part of James's and Paige's lives. In those tense first encounters, Jay spoke to Stan about God, but Stan wanted nothing to do with it. He listened, but only out of respect for Jay. In the meantime, Jay and Patte prayed and prayed. God took it over from there.

"Jay saved my life," Stan says. "His response to me was the most powerful thing that has happened in my life. He just continued and continued and never gave up on me. It made me realize that I need God. Without Him, we're all nothing, and life is just turmoil."

In his weekend visits to Bartlett, Stan began attending Mass with the two children and Jay and Patte. Gina hadn't yet signed on to return to her faith. But miraculous things were happening to Stan. He declared he wanted to convert to Catholicism. At Gina's suggestion, Jay became his sponsor for the Rite of Christian Initiation for Adults (RCIA) program. Gina, who hadn't been practicing her faith for years, returned to the Church after Paige pleaded with her to join them for Sunday Mass.

When it came time for his first confession. Stan brought notes.

"I always thought I was a man's man," Stan says, "but I cried like a baby. I was in there a long time. When I came out of there. I felt like I had lost a thousand pounds."

Exit 188 is the halfway point between Chattanooga and Memphis. Stan makes it a point to stop here, fill the tank at the mini-mart, get a soda, and stretch his legs. Outside the mini-mart, he takes a deep breath and exhales. He's feeling good.

On the seat beside him, he keeps the collection of CDs of the audio version of the *Diary of St. Faustina.* Jay gave it to him as a gift.

Pulling back on the highway, he says, "When I heard Jesus' voice on these CDs, I felt like Jesus was talking directly to me."

What struck him most is when he heard the promises Jesus made to those who pray the Chaplet of the Divine Mercy in the presence of the dying. In *Diary* entry 154, Jesus promises "I will stand between My Father and the dying person, not as the just Judge, but as the Merciful Savior."

"I got goose bumps when I heard that," Stans says.

The promises of the chaplet were what he needed to hear at a time when he needed to hear them. In 2011, within five weeks of each other, both his parents died. Stan was able to pray the chaplet at the bedside of his father on the afternoon of Aug. 6, at the moment his father took his last breath. His mother died in bed sometime between the evening of September 9 and the morning of September 10.

He had spent a lot of time with her in the weeks leading up to her death. They talked, they prayed together, including the chaplet. He hadn't planned on being in Chattanooga during this time. But a friend who has a gutter installation business gave him work in Chattanooga after a tornado ripped through town.

"God allowed me to be here for my parents in their last days," he says. "This was such a grace, such a gift."

He pauses, then says, "People die every day not having the opportunity we have to know Jesus Christ. Because we have that opportunity, it's our responsibility to share it. Now all I want to do is talk about it."

Stan and Gina — with the help of Jay and Patte — are looking to buy a home in the Memphis area to move into when they are married. In the meantime, Gina and the kids stay at her parents, and Stan visits on weekends. During the week, he continues to work as a gutter installer in Chattanooga and spends time with his boys. He gets out of work at noon on Fridays, so he can get to Memphis before he and Gina's kids go to bed.

When he and Gina look at their two beautiful children, they marvel at how God has transformed sin into love. Through those two children, God is healing a family.

"I miss them so much," he says. "It drives me bananas. I miss them so much. They're just sweethearts. What a thing to be missed by your children."

He's looking for a job in Memphis. The economy is awful. Jobs are scarce. A lot of people pray for him. He's a long way gone from the days when he made the "dollar holler." He's officially poor. He's never been more at peace.

Now an hour outside Memphis, Stan squints at the setting sun. Ironically, he's gone from selling sunglasses to installing gutters — from shading bright sunlight to redirecting rain. He'll take the sunlight. He'll take the rain. He'll take whatever God gives him. What God is giving him now is a second chance.

He calls Gina on her cell phone.

"Hi Honey. We're moving on down the road, about 60 miles out. I love you," he says. *"I'll be home soon."*

CHAPTER 11

Pornchai Moontri

Mercy Inside Those Stone Walls

Sweetest Mother, continue to teach me about the interior life. May the sword of suffering never break me. O pure Virgin, pour courage into my heart and guard it.

— Prayer of St. Faustina to the Sorrowful Mother (Diary of St. Faustina, 915)

Pornchai Moontri remembers he was carrying his knife, and he remembers struggling to get out from under the weight of a man much heavier than he. He doesn't remember much else other than that he was out of his mind from years of rage and a night of too much drinking.

But this is what authorities in Bangor, Maine, pieced together: Pornchai, a native of Thailand, stumbled into a Shop 'n Save supermarket in March 1992, proceeded to take beer from the refrigerator, open it, and drink from it. When confronted by a store manager, he tried to flee. Outside in the parking lot an altercation ensued, and a 27-year-old Shop 'n Save employee was killed with a knife wielded by Pornchai.

Pornchai was sentenced to 45 years in prison. He was 19 years old at the time. He's 39 years old today. Inside New Hampshire State Prison, Pornchi is inmate # 77948, a number not a name. But God numbers every single hair on our heads, as Pornchai has learned from Scripture (see Lk 12:7), so how much more God must cherish every single one of His children, including — and most especially — the most broken, those in most need of His mercy.

It took Pornchai years of self-righteous anger, years of self-pity, misery, and hopelessness, before he was graced with the realization that God is real, that He is Mercy Incarnate. This realization culminated when, in the prison chapel, he received the Sacraments of Baptism and Confirmation on April 10, 2010. The following day — the Feast of Divine Mercy Sunday — he received his First Holy Communion from the Most Rev. John McCormack, Bishop of Manchester, New Hampshire.

The date was no accident.

In a series of revelations to St. Maria Faustina Kowalska in the 1930s, the Lord called for this special feast day. "On that day the very depths of My tender mercy are open," Christ promised. "... The soul that will go to Confession and receive Holy Communion shall obtain complete forgiveness of sins and punishment. On that day are opened all the divine floodgates through which graces flow. Let no soul fear to draw near to Me, even though its sins be as scarlet" (*Diary of St. Faustina*, 699).

"In the course of my life," Pornchai says, "for what I have done and what has been done to me, I do need God's mercy, and He has given it to me."

That speaks volumes coming from a man who has spent more than half of his life behind bars.

✝

In a trial that lasted little more than a week, the jury sided with the prosecutor who argued that Pornchai had a "depraved indifference to the value of human life," as one press account reported.

The jury found him guilty of murder. But the jury heard nary a word about the life Pornchai led before that terrible evening. His court-appointed attorney said nothing of the victimhood Pornchai, himself, withstood long before his crime was committed. Nothing about how, two years after his birth in northern Thailand in 1973, Pornchai's mother abandoned him. Nothing about how he never attended grade school. Nothing about how his mother re-emerged with a new husband, an American, when he was 11 years old and took him to the United States against his will. Nothing was said about his assertion that his stepfather repeatedly raped him over a period of three years. Nothing about how in the racially monochromatic Maine of his youth, he was called "gook" by his classmates who did everything they could to make him feel like an outcast because of his appearance and stupid because of his broken English.

Nothing about how, at the age 14, anger was all he had.

He left home and lived on the streets of Bangor. He was placed in a school for troubled teens and promptly kicked out for fighting. He went back to living in the streets and felt it prudent to carry a knife for self-protection.

By the time he got to prison, it wasn't self-protection he sought. Rather, it was self-destruction. He was remorseful for the murder of an innocent man. He could hardly bear to think about it. Just so the pain could end, he did everything within his power to provoke fellow inmates into killing him.

"Really, I wanted them to beat me to death or stab me with a homemade knife," he says. "To me at the time, I had no reason to live."

Because of his violent tendencies, Pornchai was placed into solitary confinement many times for a combined six-plus years. What that often meant was spending 23 hours a day alone in a tiny cell. On his first day in "solitary," he entered the cell, and it was so filthy he took the advice of a neighboring inmate to set off the fire sprinklers in order to hose the cell down. It worked, more or less, but it also prompted the first of many instances whereby he was pulled from his cell and subdued by men in full riot gear, his limbs bent backwards nearly to the point of snapping.

He slept on a cement cot. He had 45 minutes of recreation time per day where he was brought to a five-feet wide by eight-feet-long chain-link cage. He was given a dab of toothpaste each day to brush his teeth using his finger. He was not permitted to have a toothbrush. Is it possible to kill oneself with a toothbrush? He probably would have tried if given the chance. Without a second thought, Pornchai would have cut an artery or hung himself if he had the means.

He had access to three books per week. He chose the thickest in order to make them last. Those books included a peculiar combination of Stephen King novels and the Bible, which he said he read cover to cover twice. Pornchai could relate to the horror, violence, and psychological depravity depicted by Stephen King in novels often set in — of all places — small-town Maine. As for relating to the Bible — not so much. Hope and salvation were the stuff of fiction, not much different than a haunted 1958 Plymouth Fury in the King novel *Christine* or the monster lurking in a small town's sewers in *IT*. Still, anything that could help drown out the madness of prison life and that of his own mind was worth the effort.

"Inmates would do anything to try to break up their day and entertain themselves," Pornchai says. "Some played with their own urine and feces, and others used those as weapons, throwing them at the guards after calling their names to get their attention."

He says he survived those early years of his incarceration by doing push-ups — as many as 1,500 a day — "and venting as much of my anger, frustration, and energy as possible into physical fitness."

He says, "In a way, this also worked against me. The more physically strong I became, the more I was treated like a dangerous animal."

It was in solitary confinement where he learned of the death of his mother. She was murdered, in Guam, where she had relocated.

"I was now alone in my rage," Pornchai says.

When he finally was released for good from solitary confinement, he says, he had at least as many psychological problems as the day he entered prison.

"I was angry, depressed, often hostile, and anti-social," he says.

He was transferred from the prison in Maine to New Hampshire State Prison, and he viewed the transfer as an opportunity for "a new beginning." He was placed within the general prison population, and his urge to commit violence had subsided. Eventually, he formed a friendship that changed his life.

It was with a Catholic priest.

✝

Through a fellow inmate, Pornchai met the Rev. Gordon MacRae, a down-to-earth, straightforward spiritual man and prolific writer who seemed to have a lot of answers to a lot of questions. *Is there a God? Who is He? How can we be sure? Why should we trust?*

Father Gordon, 59, was convicted in 1994 on five sexual assault counts that have since been called into question, including by *The Wall Street Journal* whose two-part series in 2005 brought national attention to his case. He has had wide public support for his cause, including from the late Cardinal Avery Dulles, who encouraged Fr. Gordon to continue writing, which he does through a website, thesestonewalls.com, administered by a friend from outside of prison.

Pornchai had no idea who he was dealing with, and he and Fr. Gordon's first meetings were not particularly transcendent. Rather, they were all business.

"I was real hostile and told [Fr. Gordon] I just wanted him to help me get transferred to a prison in Bangkok, Thailand," Pornchai says.

Father Gordon told him to be careful what he asked for. "I won't help you pursue something that will only further destroy you," he said.

Pornchai was bewildered by this guy.

"I didn't care if I would be 'destroyed,'" Pornchai recalls, "so why on earth should Gordon care? I was hostile to him for a long time. I had mastered the art of driving anyone who cared away from me, but in Gordon, I had met my match."

Indeed, in contrast to just about every inmate with whom Pornchai had come into contact, Fr. Gordon wanted nothing from him. Not a thing. And to boot, he didn't thump his Bible, and he didn't judge. He was — well — *nice*, a trait in short supply in prison.

How peculiar that was for Pornchai. What a stark contrast to the loss and emptiness in his own life. Still, turning with trust to another person carried great risks. Why? Because trust could leave Pornchai vulnerable. He had spent most of his life standing in the debris of some form of broken trust. Trust in his family. Trust in his peers. Trust in the justice system. Trust in himself. He had learned long ago not to trust anyone or anything. It was too risky. Plus, he was still acclimating to his "new beginning," his sharp transformation from depression, anxiety, self-hate, guilt, and fear. He was still adjusting from a life of misery to one of mere unhappiness.

Within a few months of meeting Fr. Gordon, Pornchai was moved into the same unit as his. The two became fast friends and eventually cellmates — and the trust blossomed.

"By patience and especially by example, Gordon helped me change the course of my life," Pornchai says. "He is my best friend and the person I trust most in this world."

✝

The two share a 96-square-feet cell that serves as living room, bedroom, kitchen, and toilet. The cell's built-in mirror sits over the sink. The mirror is warped, like one of those carnival fun-house mirrors. In the morning, when they lean into it to wash or shave, their faces look misshapen. In a way, it's a cruel joke. In prison, you are condemned to hold the proverbial mirror to yourself. And if you're not careful, a distorted self-image stares right back at you.

Pornchai doesn't fall for it anymore. For him now, a warped mirror is just a warped mirror, another indignity of prison life. Besides, when he leans in close enough — to his own reflection, to his own heart — the distortion diminishes. He can see himself the way others now see him. Eyes that once smoldered with coiled rage now sparkle with purpose and compassion. He laughs when he describes the reaction he gets now from prisoners who knew him back before his conversion.

"They now see a man who, despite the pain and difficulty of being in prison, is at peace," he says.

Pornchai says Fr. Gordon never pushed him into becoming Catholic.

"He never even brought it up," Pornchai says. "I was pulled to it by the force of grace and the hope that one day I could do good for others."

Through Fr. Gordon, Pornchai discovered the saints and the Blessed Mother. In the saints, particularly Maximilian Kolbe, he discovered what it means to truly be a man, what it means to be tough. Toughness isn't carrying a knife and brandishing it against those he perceives as a threat. Toughness isn't getting beaten to the point of near death and not caring about it. A man doesn't seek to destroy other men. A man doesn't hold his own needs above the needs of others. A real man is selfless. In St. Maximilian Kolbe, who certainly knew what it was like to be stripped of his humanity and dignity, Pornchai finds recourse because Kolbe never caved in to despair. He professed his love for God, and there was no pussyfooting around about it. In 1941, at Auschwitz, he gave his life to save that of another man.

That's manhood. That's tough. And that's why Pornchai took the name Maximilian as his Christian name when he was baptized. Modeling himself on Maximilian, Pornchai now reaches out to fellow prisoners who are having a difficult time, including those in danger from other inmates. Some prison guards now steer vulnerable inmates toward Pornchai and Fr. Gordon.

"They know that we'll show them the ropes and how to do the right things to avoid creating hardship for themselves, for other inmates, and for the guards," says Pornchai.

In the Blessed Mother, Pornchai discovered what it means to say yes to God. She is his "Mama Mary." When the archangel tells Mary that she is to bear the Son of God and name Him Jesus, she surrenders herself completely to the Divine plan: "Behold, I am the handmaid of the Lord; let it be to me according to your word" (Lk 1:38). She says yes, despite the implications for her future — her life's plans would be shattered. Yes, despite the danger to her — a Jewish woman pregnant out of wedlock could be stoned to death. Yes, despite the awesome responsibility — the call to be the Mother of the Son of God, the Savior of the world.

That's faith. That's no fooling around.

Even when surrounded by doubters, Mary remained steadfast in her faith — including at the most critical moment, on Calvary, when promises made at the Annunciation didn't seem to be coming true.

Was such acceptance of God's will easy? No, and it isn't for Pornchai either. But he did things his own way for years, and where did that lead? After all he went through, surrendering to God only made sense. He could surrender all those fears and all the burdens he had carried. He could accept that while society has judged him, God hasn't.

Pornchai and Fr. Gordon keep religious images on their cell walls, including of the Blessed Virgin Mary, St. Maximilian Kolbe, and the Divine Mercy image of Jesus.

Through Jesus Himself and through these holy servants of the Lord — more rewarding than through that warped mirror — they lean in and seek their own reflections in Christ.

✝

Pornchai has immersed himself in religious studies. He earned his Graduate Equivalency Diploma (GED). He's excellent at detailed carpentry, including building model ships. He lives a life of prayer and performs deeds of mercy. Gifted in math, Pornchai tutors inmates who also seek to obtain their high school equivalency diplomas.

Fellow inmate, Donald Spinner, a Catholic convert, says his faith took root through Pornchai's example.

"Pornchai, especially, has influenced so many people here," he says. "We all expect Father G. to be a good person, but Pornchai's life of grace is inspiring to everyone. ... The cost of discipleship for me has been the loss of my selfishness. No one can be selfish in such company."

For Fr. Gordon, Pornchai has been an inspiration, a blessing from God that has helped him on his own difficult journey.

"I have never met a man more determined to live the faith he has professed than Pornchai Moontri," Fr. Gordon says. "In the darkness and aloneness of a prison cell night after night for the last two of his 20 years in prison, Pornchai has stared down the anxiety of uncertainty, he has struggled for reasons to believe, and he has found them."

✝

In less than two years, Pornchai will be eligible for a commutation or reduction in his sentence. He prays for his release. It would at least give him enough time to start a new life at a relatively young age. Still, when given his freedom, he is to be immediately deported back to Thailand, a place he hasn't been to since he was 11 and whose language he never learned to read and write. He hasn't even heard Thai spoken for more than 25 years.

Moreover, he has no connections there.

He'll step off the plane — then what?

The only thing he's sure of is that he will step upon the land where he was born, having experienced a rebirth. From there, he hopes to serve in a ministry helping troubled youth.

"From age 11 to 32, I always felt I was alone, that no one cared and no one loved me," Pornchai says. "I want to be able to help those who are struggling like I did. I ask in my prayers every night that God will use me as an instrument. That's what I look forward to."

CHAPTER 12

Fred Berretta

'God, Be Merciful to Us'

Jesus to St. Faustina:

This is the hour of great mercy. ...
In this hour, I will refuse nothing
to the soul that makes a request
of Me in virtue of My Passion.

— Diary of St. Faustina, 1320

A banker on a business trip in New York City, Fred Berretta had just checked into his hotel room. He had about 20 minutes down time before he had to meet his colleagues.

For some reason, he decided to clean out his briefcase, something he hadn't done in a long time. As he emptied it out, he came across a booklet he had stuffed into a pocket years ago on praying the Chaplet of the Divine Mercy. He recalls having prayed it a few times years ago. But by January 15, 2009, it was a good intention mislaid among spreadsheets and quarterly reports and matters that seemed far more pressing.

Only two weeks prior, Fred had made a New Year's resolution to try to get into better spiritual shape. Here in this hotel room was an opportunity to fulfill it. So he followed along in the booklet and prayed the Chaplet of the Divine Mercy, a prayer Jesus gave to St. Maria Faustina Kowalska.

He prayed slowly and with great intensity, in a way that was unusual for him:

For the sake of His sorrowful Passion,
have mercy on us and on the whole world.

The time happened to be 3 o'clock, known as the Hour of Great Mercy, when Jesus died on the cross. Fred would consider that detail the following day — as he was preparing to die.

He would be among the 155 people to board a jet airliner at LaGuardia Airport bound for Charlotte, North Carolina, his hometown. Ninety seconds after takeoff, the jet would hit a flock of geese, the engines would explode, and the plane would lose power at 3,200 feet. The aircraft would be out of reach from any airfield. It would lose thrust and altitude. Everything would become eerily quiet. Fred would cinch his seatbelt. His left hand would clutch the armrest, his heart would race, his face would be flush.

He would think about his family — his wife and four young children. He would think about God, about death, about trust, about an extraordinary promise made by Jesus that he had read the previous day in that booklet.

"*Prepare for impact*," the pilot would say over the PA system.

What was the promise? Suddenly, it would come to him, the last passage he read before heading off to his meeting. Jesus said to St. Faustina, "This is the hour of great mercy. ... In this hour, I will refuse nothing to the soul that makes a request of Me in virtue of My Passion (*Diary of St. Faustina*, 1320).

As the ground surged into view, Fred would look at his watch. It would be 3:30 p.m., the Hour of Great Mercy!

"I prayed with every fiber of emotion and sincerity I could muster, 'God, please be merciful to us,'" Fred would recall two weeks later.

Most people have heard about the crash landing of Flight 1549 in the Hudson River on January 15, 2009. No one was seriously injured. Politicians and news anchors quickly dubbed it the "Miracle on the Hudson." In the history of aviation, no jet airliner had ever made an emergency landing on water without casualties.

Then, there were the news images. Around the world, people saw the remarkable sight of the U.S. Airways Airbus floating gently down the frigid Hudson, like some sort of breaching, people-friendly, aquatic creature. The passengers stood on its wings, calmly awaiting rescue. Amidst all the news of economic collapse, of tens of thousands of layoffs on a weekly basis, of families in peril, of a reckoning at hand for a culture of greed, this plane, these passengers, its pilot — all served as a sort of restorative balm on our nation's collective consciousness.

The story made you gasp, gulp hard, smile widely, and be thankful. Thankful for what? For *good* news. For heroes in the pilot, Chesley "Sully" Sullenberger, and the rest of the crew. Thankful in the knowledge that in the panic-filled moments when the plane lurched to a stop, it wasn't every man and woman for him or herself. Thankful that humanity's better nature was on display. Thankful the incident wasn't terrorist-related, but rather geese-related. Thankful that a guy like Fred Berretta, 41 at the time, would live to walk through the door of his home once again, hug his wife and children, and make sure they knew he loved them — that he always had and that he always will.

✝

For devotees of Divine Mercy, Flight 1549 serves as further proof that the Lord keeps His promises.

We may never have learned Fred Berretta's story if it weren't for a man named Vinny Flynn. Following the crash, Fred felt compelled to send an e-mail of thanks to Vinny. Though Vinny and his family are seen daily at 3 p.m. (EST) on EWTN singing the Chaplet of the Divine Mercy from the National Shrine of The Divine Mercy in Stockbridge, Fred had never heard of Vinny until about two hours before he boarded Flight 1549.

Following morning meetings on January 15, Fred found himself in the unusual position of having some free time on a business trip. It was noon. He stepped inside Manhattan's St. Patrick's Cathedral. He stayed for the noon Mass. Afterwards, he lit a candle in a side chapel and went into St. Patrick's gift shop. A book caught his eye — Vinny's *7 Secrets of the Eucharist* (Mercy Song Ignatius Press, 2006), which, with citations from St. Faustina's *Diary*, gives a greater understanding of the mystery of the Eucharist. It was not a large book. He figured he could read it in one sitting, perfect for a two-hour flight.

Here's what happened next: "I got into a cab and went to the airport," he said. "My flight was delayed about 15 minutes, so I sat there and started reading Vinny's book. I was really taken by it. I boarded the plane and continued to read. As I read, I became engrossed in the book and was thinking about how meager my spiritual life had been before over the years. Just as we were rolling out for takeoff, I put the book away and closed my eyes. The plane lifted off Runway 4, and as we climbed, I heard the sound of the landing gear retracting, followed by the clunk of the gear tucking itself into the wings. I was feeling relaxed. My mind moved back and forth between work, my family, the noon Mass at St. Patrick's, and on what I had been reading. " Then, I heard the impact and, with it, a violent jolt, then the explosion, and the plane shook violently."

Fred was sitting in seat 16A, which is behind the left wing. He could see the dark, foul-looking trail of smoke coming out of the left engine. Then fire, and then he could smell the jet fuel.

Fred grew up under the flight path of an airport. He loved planes. As a boy, he would lay out in his backyard for hours watching the planes on their descent. He could tell you the makes and models of all of them. He eventually got his pilot's license. As he looked out the window from seat 16A, he became increasingly alarmed, but he tried to remain calm. Provided the engine didn't explode or the wing itself catch fire, he knew that all twin-engine commercial airliners, including the Airbus A-320, could fly on one engine.

The flight crew said nothing over the intercom, but as he felt the plane start to level off and make a left hand turn — gradual, then more pronounced — it was clear the pilot was preparing for an emergency landing.

"I kept telling myself, 'Okay, we've lost the left engine, and we're going to make an emergency landing. We still have the right engine, and we'll be fine,'" Fred recalls.

But as the plane leveled off, he says, "I heard something else I had never heard on a plane before: silence. There was no engine roar or vibration, just the faintest hint of the wind passing by outside, and perhaps a very slight puffing noise, ever so soft, coming from the left engine."

He got the attention of a man on the other side of the aisle.

"What's going on over there?" he asked him. "Can you see anything? Is the right engine making noise? Can you hear anything?"

The man looked out the window and then back. "I don't hear anything," he said.

Fred heard some cries from the cabin. He could feel the descent. He could see Manhattan below looming larger and larger until the aircraft was level with the rooftops. Sweat broke out across his face and body.

"Some of us looked at each other," he said. "There was nothing to be said. I knew that the only thing I could do was pray."

These were the other things he knew: This sleek, high performance jet airliner had suddenly and irreversibly become a 73-ton glider, sinking fast above one of the nation's most densely populated regions. It would touch down somewhere, somehow, very soon, at a speed of about 120 miles per hour. The chances of survival were almost nil.

He thought about his family, how hard his death would be on them. Indeed, that was the most painful part of the experience for him, his concern for them. His life didn't flash before his eyes, per se. "I thought about my life holistically — as a boy, an adolescent, and a man," he says. "I assimilated a mini self-judgment and life review."

✝

Growing up, his family was "nominally Catholic" — they attended Mass most Sundays, but prayer at home was rarely emphasized. Around the time of his eighth birthday, his parents announced to him and his two older sisters that they would be separating. He stayed with his mother, while his sisters went to live with their father. They all remained in Florida. Fred was moved around a lot from town to town and school to school. The stability of his younger years had crumbled. He spent a lot of time on his own. He read a lot.

By the time he moved in with his father, he no longer attended Mass, and he rarely prayed. As a boy, he would hear the voice of God speaking to his heart. But now as a teen, he no longer listened. In college, his relationship with God came only in fits and starts until it was reduced to merely blaming God for the things that went wrong in his life and in the world. Yet, on the positive side: He still *believed*.

Upon his marriage to Liz, he felt renewed in his faith. But the spiritual high didn't last. He allowed career, and the pressures therein, to get in the way.

On board Flight 1549, he thought about the very thing that seemed to stand in the way of growing deeper in his faith for all these years. It came down to this: trust. He didn't have much. Ever. He had once fancied himself among the titans of commerce in an era of young Wall Street superstars. He once trusted that money would bring security and peace of mind.

This flight wasn't the thing that taught him otherwise. Rather, it was the past year. The bottom fell out of the economy, and with it, much of Fred's savings of the last 20 years.

By Christmas, the self-described "half-hearted Catholic" knew in his heart the only security in the world is the security found in God, which led to his New Year's resolution; which led to him praying the chaplet in a hotel room; which led him to buy Vinny's book; which led him to close his eyes in seat 16A, his trajectory heavenward. He began to reflect upon how God is real and He loves us and that He wants us to turn to Him in trust.

Which is exactly what Fred did when he suddenly realized it was the Hour of Great Mercy, knowing he would probably be dead in a matter of seconds. He trusted, truly, for the first time.

All these fragments of thought seemed to piece themselves into place. The plane was going down, yet everything was making sense. He admits he was in shock. But he also felt peace — a deep peace. God had allowed him to find the Divine Mercy booklet in his briefcase. God had allowed him time to go to Mass at noon and receive Holy Communion. God had steered him to Vinny's book. God did all this, he thought, to prepare him for death.

He hunched over in his seat to brace for impact. He prayed for God's mercy. Then, he prayed two Hail Marys and one Our Father. He made it halfway though a prayer to St. Michael, the Archangel, when the plane hit the water, came to a stop, and bobbed up and down like a toy in a kiddy pool.

✝

"Under the most precarious of situations I could ever imagine," says Fred, "God taught me what true peace is all about — that it's found in accepting God's will. That we must try our best in this life, but not sweat the small stuff, and hand control over to God. The 'Miracle on the Hudson' was, for me, a grace confirming that I must commit to God fully and live my faith wholeheartedly, doing the best I can in life in all I do and leaving the rest to God."

One more thing to mention. A couple weeks before the flight, Fred had prayed the Rosary for the first time in years. He had recently learned of the 15 promises that, as a certain tradition has it, the Virgin Mary made to St. Dominic and Blessed Alan to all who pray the Rosary with a faithful heart. Fred remembers thinking at the time, "Are those promises real?" He feels he recently received his answer.

"I still have my boarding pass from the flight," he said, "and I couldn't help but to notice all the 15s associated with the flight. We left on January 15, from gate 15. It was Flight 1549, with 155 passengers. Also, it took off during the 15th hour, by military time, which is what the world of aviation uses. I smiled when it hit me later. There was my answer right there."

He's vowed to embrace the Eucharist, thanks to Vinny; the Rosary, thanks to all those 15s; and the Chaplet of Divine Mercy, thanks to that booklet.

God was doing more than preparing him for death: God was preparing him for life.

Felix Carroll

CHAPTER 13

Fr. Jack Fullen

'The Stupid Servant'

Jesus to St. Faustina:

The greatest misery does not stop Me from uniting Myself to a soul, but where there is pride, I am not there.

— Diary of St Faustina, 1563

He had only one request for this story on him. "Please title it, 'The Stupid Servant,'" he said. So there it is.

Stupid? He wasn't the best student. Yeah, but *stupid?* He wasn't always the most faithful Catholic. But then God lovingly hit him upside the head.

Introducing Fr. Jack Fullen — living proof of the intercessory power of Our Lady of Lourdes who brought Fr. Jack to the feett of Jesus, the Divine Mercy. He's not stupid. Maybe, in retrospect, he's just thickheaded.

Raised into poverty in Brooklyn, the young Jack Fullen made a brash prediction to his future bride two nights before their wedding in 1962. (Yes, he was married.) "I promised Sandy I would make a million dollars before I was 30 years old," he says.

He was 22 at the time.

By the age of 30, he wasn't a millionaire. Instead, he was diagnosed with cancer. God had a different plan for him.

The first time he laid eyes on Sandy was at college in Connecticut. It was a Saturday night. He was heading back to his dorm. He saw her, a blond, beautiful girl. She was getting out of a car, and she looked angry.

"I looked at her and thought to myself, 'I'm going to marry that girl,'" he recalls. "I didn't even know who she was."

In a nutshell, this is who she was: Raised Episcopalian, Sandy was decidedly headstrong in all things, including her faith. Physically, she was stunning. She was filled with verve.

In a nutshell, this is who Jack was: Raised Catholic, he had drifted from his faith. He was ambitious. He was friendly and charming, and people liked him, particularly Sandy.

Following graduation and then their wedding, he officially became "a man," as he says, as a result of three factors: He joined the U.S. Marine Corps, he became a husband, and then he became a father. Pam was their first child. He was smitten. He wept with joy when he held Pam for the first time.

Jack eventually parlayed his military experience as a communications officer into a career in the private sector. The salary

was fantastic. Sandy and Jack had a son, Michael. By all accounts
— except spiritually — Jack Fullen was a successful man. But by
all accounts — except spiritually — things would soon come
crashing down.

On Nov. 15, 1969, at the age of 29, he felt a lump on his
neck. He was diagnosed with Hodgkin's disease, a form of
cancer of the lymphatic system. This is what happened next:

Sandy panicked.
He was fired from his job.
They slipped into poverty.
Their third child, Jason, was on the way.

"When you have a spiritual life, bad things that happen are
not devastating," he says. "When you don't have a spiritual life,
which I didn't at the time, these things are devastating."

He turned 30, a year in which he would not become a
millionaire. He went into a deep depression. Then, Sandy
encouraged him to attend a communications trade show. A
company from Washington, D.C., hired him. The company,
apparently, had misunderstood the term "Hodgkin's disease."

"They must have thought Hodgkin's was heartburn," he
says, with a laugh.

This was 1971. He and the family were now living in D.C.
He was still undergoing cancer treatment. While his career was
back on track, he continually felt death following him around.
By 1973, his marriage was a wreck. He hardly gave his children
his attention.

Sandy convinced him to attend a Marriage Encounter
weekend. It opened a spiritual door. He went to confession,
the first time in at least 12 years. The weekend brought Jack
and Sandy to new heights in their relationship *and* with God.
At the closing of the weekend, they attended Mass. He was
filled with joy that he could receive Holy Communion. When
he got back to the pew, Sandy was crying. She wanted to receive
Jesus, too, but she wasn't Catholic, so she knew she couldn't.
Not yet, anyway.

After the weekend, she kept pushing Jack to talk about God. Her insistence intimidated him. One night, she came running up the stairs and jumped on him in the bed and pounded on him and called him all kinds of names. "You *promised*, you promised that tonight we would talk," she said. He pushed her off of him. He stood up on the bed in just his boxer shorts and started screaming at her.

"Sand, you are a better 'Catholic' than I have ever been!" he yelled. "You've taken the kids to church while I've been in bed. You've taken them to CCD. You've instructed them in Catholicism. Get off of my [*bleep*] back and call Fr. Brooks and make an appointment to become Catholic and leave me alone!"

He laid back down, pulled the covers up to his eyes, and thought, "Wow, I just made an ass of myself." Sandy laid down beside him and whispered in his ear. "Thank you," she said. "I have been waiting for that invitation for 11 years."

She made the appointment with Fr. Brooks, who was shocked she *wasn't* Catholic. She certainly seemed Catholic. In 1974, she became Catholic.

There were three things Sandy had a problem with, like most Protestants:

1. The Sacrament of Reconciliation
2. The Blessed Mother
3. The Holy Father.

Her doubts about each would be overcome soon enough. She went to confession and felt freed. She went to Rome and felt a love for the leader of the worldwide Church. The Blessed Mother was a more complicated matter.

Meanwhile, in 1975, Jack's cancer had spread to below his diaphragm. He was undergoing chemotherapy. While the tumor had shrunk, it was still the size of a large orange. The doctors recommended radiation treatment to be undergone at Sloan-Kettering Cancer Center in New York. Jack refused.

It was a jubilee year for the Church. By then, Jack and Sandy had become Marriage Encounter counselors, and they were organizing a pilgrimage to Rome. Jack knew if he started the treatment, he wouldn't be able to go. His doctors were upset. Still, he left on a pilgrimage that changed his life.

Instead of going directly to Rome, the group decided to stop first in Lourdes, France, site of the Marian apparitions to St. Bernadette. Neither Sandy nor Jack was enthused about the Lourdes leg of the pilgrimage. For Sandy, even though she had converted to Catholicism, she didn't want to engage in what she considered "idolatry" of the Blessed Mother. She saw devotion to the Blessed Mother as taking away from God. Jack, himself, viewed devotion to the Blessed Mother as "hokum and a lot of superstition." In Lourdes, the plan was that they would remain in the hotel room until it was time to go to Rome.

It didn't work out according to plan.

They made their way down to the famous grotto. The place was pandemonium. But after walking through St. Joseph's Gate, they both felt an indescribable serenity.

"I had never felt such peace since I was diagnosed with Hodgkin's," says Jack. "All the pressure, all of the depression, just drained from me."

The next morning, he and Sandy made their way down to the baths, where many healings have been reported since Our Lady appeared to St. Bernadette in 1858. Jack soon noticed something peculiar. Everyone had rosaries, and they didn't.

They bought rosaries — just to fit in. Once queued up to enter the baths, Jack asked, "Are you going to go in?" Sandy said, "No, the baths are not for me, they're for you." Once inside, Jack undressed down to his skivvies. As he stood in the baths, he looked out and could see Sandy in the distance, and she was praying the Rosary.

"And I remember thinking, 'If there's any miracle that's going to happen, *there it is.* That's a miracle, that my Protestant bride who wanted nothing to do with the Blessed Mother is praying the Rosary!'" After he stepped out of the baths, he couldn't find Sandy. He waited and waited.

"Then, all the sudden, out of the crowd comes this blond bombshell, screaming, 'You're cured! You're cured!'"

recalled Jack. "She jumps on me and hugs me and screams, 'You're cured!'

"I was devastated because I had no belief I was cured. None whatsoever. I thought, 'She's now going to lose her faith. I'm going to go back to New York, I'll still have the cancer. I'll do the radiation. She's completely flipped out.'

"So I tell her, 'Stop screaming, stop screaming.' Then, we link up with our friends, and she's still screaming, 'Jack's cured! Jack's cured! We have to go to Rome and thank Jesus for his cure.'"

When they returned to the United States, the first thing Jack had to do was go to George Washington Hospital in Washington for a series of X-rays to determine the extent of the disease. The appointment was supposed to last an hour, and then Jack was to fly to New York for treatment at Sloane Kettering. The appointment lasted three hours. He missed his plane. They took so many X-rays that Jack assumed the cancer had spread. He became worried. He demanded to see a doctor.

The radiologist finally came in. He was Jewish. He started putting up a series of X-rays taken of Jack over several years. Jack had no clue what he was looking at. Black is good, white is not good, or is it the other way around? Then, the radiologist posted the X-rays of that day and asked, "Mr. Fullen, tell me, what *don't* you see?"

"I don't understand what I'm supposed to be seeing or not seeing," Jack said.

"Well, I'll tell you what you *don't* see," the radiologist said. "You don't see the tumor." The radiologist then paused for a moment. "So, where have you been?" he asked Jack.

"Nowhere," Jack responded.

"Mr. Fullen," the radiologist said, "you should still have the tumor. Besides which, you should have *more* tumors. So, Mr. Fullen, where have you been?"

Saint Peter denied Jesus three times. Jack denied the Blessed Mother twice.

Again, Jack said, "Nowhere."

The radiologist called him a "mashugana," which is Yiddish for "idiot."

"Then, he throws me out of his office. He wouldn't even give me the X-rays," Jack recalled.

"You don't need the X-rays," the radiologist said.

"I have to go to New York!" Jack protested.

"You don't have to go to New York! If you want to go to New York, go to New York, but I am calling Sloan Kettering and canceling the radiation. It's gone. It's a miracle."

Jack was infuriated with him. He could not imagine the tumor was not there. "I took the elevator back down and stepped outside and saw the sky," Jack recalls. "There was the most beautiful blue sky you could ever imagine, and the Blessed Mother spoke to my heart and said, 'You're cured.' At that moment, I felt complete exhilaration and joy."

He had to talk to someone. He called home.

"Sandy! Sandy!" he said. "They can't find the tumor! They can't find the tumor! The Blessed Mother told me I'm cured!"

"I knew that, you idiot!" Sandy said. Then, she proceeded to give him a list of things she needed from the grocery store.

✝

The non-millionaire Jack Fullen's whole drive for success and career stopped. God used him and Sandy to evangelize and bring people to Jesus through weekend Marriage Encounters. But that was only the beginning of an extraordinary spiritual journey.

In 1981, Jack attended Mass at the Basilica of the National Shrine of the Immaculate Conception in Washington, D.C. After Mass, he prayed the Rosary, asking the Blessed Mother to lead Sandy and him into the next phase of their lives.

"Then, I had this incredible voice within me say, 'You are to become a priest.' I couldn't believe it," he recalls. "I thought, 'This is stupid. This is crazy. I'm married. I have children!' I thought, 'This is diabolical.'" He never told Sandy about the experience. But something inside of him changed. He began reading spiritual books. Sometimes, he'd even peek at vocation pamphlets.

On a vacation Sandy and Jack made to Germany, Sandy came down with a cold. Her cold got significantly worse. In the city of Mannheim, she was diagnosed with pneumonia in both lungs. That night was the last time she received Jesus in the Eucharist.

"I remember before she received Jesus, she said the Our Father," he says, "and she was like a little girl sitting on the edge of the bed. She had tubes on her nose for oxygen, and I remember her saying the Protestant doxology, 'For Thine is the kingdom and the power and the glory ... .' It was like she was going back in time."

The next day, her medical team had to induce a coma because she had developed adult respiratory distress syndrome, which is almost always fatal in adults. The ventilator shredded her lungs. Air filled her torso. She was dying.

Jack had a flashback to that day in the Basilica. "God, You were right," he thought. "You do have a plan for me to become a priest. *Really*? Is that *really* Your plan?"

In the midst of his sorrow, God gave him the grace to know He would bring good from all this suffering.

Jack went to the hospital chapel. Under a statue of the Blessed Virgin Mary, he sobbed uncontrollably. A priest came to him and held him and comforted him. Back in Sandy's room, he could hardly recognize her. She was in her last moments. Jack laid down in bed with her and held her and began praying the Glorious Mysteries of the Rosary. He wanted to give Sandy to Jesus and the Blessed Mother through the Glorious Mysteries, specifically. But when he finished, she hadn't died yet. So he prayed the Joyful Mysteries, and she didn't die. He didn't want to pray the Sorrowful Mysteries because her suffering was almost over. But he *had* to pray them because, as he says, "I'm a male, and I have to complete things."

Sandy died on the fourth Sorrowful Mystery, the Carrying of the Cross.

"I fell on the floor and kept yelling at God internally, saying, 'Why? Why now on the fourth Sorrowful Mystery? Why did you take her on the fourth Sorrowful Mystery?'" he recalls. "And I heard in my heart, 'It's not *her* cross, it's *your* cross.' I felt like a knife was inserted in my torso and I was split in half, that the two that had become one was torn and it was only me."

But then by the time Jack got back to his feet, he was filled with joy.

"I knew she was OK," he says.

He had a vision of her standing by his side. They were sharing things so intimately, things about God and themselves and about how much love God has for us all. It was a moment "out of time," he says. "Her soul leaving her body was so profound. She was standing next to me and sharing, and I couldn't understand why the others in the room were so persistent that she was dead. And I was saying, 'She's standing here with me!' Through an interpreter, they told me to leave so they could take out the tubes, then I could come back and say goodbye to her. I said, 'Why? She's not there.' I kept pointing to her body. I was dumbfounded."

He brought Sandy's body home. Together with his three kids, he buried her.

✝

When his youngest, Jason, was old enough to be on his own, Jack worked and prayed his way into the priesthood and was ordained at the Cathedral of Mary, Our Queen, in Baltimore, Maryland, on May 27, 1995, the day after Sandy's birthday. After retiring from active ministry in the Archdiocese of Baltimore, he became a resident in the Arlington Diocese where he co-founded the Missionaries of Our Lady of Divine Mercy, which is dedicated to serving the poor through the spiritual and corporal works of mercy.

"Our Blessed Mother brought me to Jesus, the Divine Mercy," Fr. Jack says. "He was there waiting for me the whole time, I know it. It's just like you see Him in that image of Divine Mercy, which shows Him stepping out towards us. We see how Divine Mercy changes lives. It's a very slow, powerful, fermenting action of God for the world — an intervention that's causing people to return to God. It's not about a lot of 'hoopla.' It's about saving one soul at a time. This is the will of God, to do works of mercy, to strive for holiness."

Father Jack Fullen died May 7, 2010, from heart disease.

He once said, "The finest moment of my life is to see the face of God — His loving face. And the second was to see the face of Sandy."

Felix Carroll

CHAPTER 14

Mary Cooke

A Harrowing Search for Home

I see everything differently now.
I am conscious of what the Lord, by
one single word, has done in my soul,
and I live by it. ... I would not have
believed that one could suffer so, if
I had not gone through it myself.

— Diary of St. Faustina, 104

"I am a spiritual person, not a religious person, a *spiritual* person," Mary Cooke would often hear herself say. It is a claim often heard from people searching for meaning in their lives — searching for God. In Mary's case, what became a harrowing spiritual journey says as much about what can go terribly wrong under misguided spiritual tutelage — Catholic spiritual tutelage included — and what can go right when the search for truth ends in the Heart of the Merciful Savior.

First things first. Here's how things can go terribly wrong.

A cradle Catholic, she was six years old when a nun brought her first grade class down to the basement of the school, opened the furnace, and pointed to the flames. Sister explained that's what hell looks like. She said that bad children could expect to take up permanent residency in similarly inhospitable lodgings. The God about whom Mary learned was a God of anger. The adults who instructed her were typically condemnatory. There was no talk of God's mercy. No talk of Jesus' mission to save poor sinners. No talk of how His love for us is greater than any sin.

Then, there was Mary's fear of death. She was in fourth grade when her best friend died from a heart defect. Put at the front of the line when her class was lead to the girl's open casket, Mary was told by her teacher to place her hand on the dead child's head, so that she could clearly understand her friend was no longer alive. The forehead was waxy from the embalmment. Mary nearly passed out. A nun tried to calm her, telling her that death is just like sleep.

For months afterward, Mary would lie awake in bed afraid to fall asleep. Putting her small hand on her mother's forehead, she would wake her mother up in the middle of the night to make sure she was still alive. Still, Mary loved Catholic ritual — the Mass, the music, the incense, the reverence — and she loved singing in the choir.

But as she grew into her teen years — what she describes as "massively tumultuous years" — her family life grew toxic, and Mary became progressively rebellious. The Church was one of the first casualties. She was repulsed by the inconsistencies of many Christians who professed brotherly love but didn't practice it. The confessional was to be a place of peace and healing, but her priest once ripped into her when she confessed that she had lied to her mother.

Mary says, "I definitely was no angel. I know that. But I wanted to have a conversation with him, to tell him how things seemed so disordered, and instead he started yelling at me." She did her penance — 10 Our Fathers.

Then, she was gone.

"I am going to find the God of love and kindness I know exists — somewhere," Mary thought to herself.

She spent the next 30 years in search of meaning and proof for a higher power, or an inner power for that matter: something that would take away the brokenness and despair, some path to self-improvement and self-empowerment. *Something.* If she was at full simmer in seeking the truth when she left home at 17, she soon cooled herself down by buying into the promises of a more relativistic age.

It was the early 1970s. The old rules were erased. The Church and its teachings had already lost much of its influence in American culture. This young generation, if they thought of the Church at all, typically either cannibalized its teachings for spare parts (its call for social justice, for instance, or its command to love thy neighbor) or discarded it all together (certainly beginning with its teachings on sexuality, virtue, contraception, and the Holy Trinity).

"God" was merely "energy" or simply a foundational principle or an idea — not a person, not a divinity. Drug use was rampant. And anyone well learned in comparative religion and psychology, anyone with a fair amount of charm, charisma, and self-esteem, could hang a shingle and call him or herself a healer, a guru, an enlightened master, or a shaman. Many did and still do — some well-intentioned souls and others who are outright con artists.

Mary mingled with both types. She smoked pot, but she was no flower child. She finished college and taught children with disabilities. Mary married and had a baby girl. She described herself then as "relatively conservative." She baptized her child

Episcopalian after her husband's religious preference, and they all attended weekly Sunday services. They redecorated their old colonial house in an upper-class neighborhood in Massachusetts. During the summers, they sailed the East Coast on their 40-foot yawl and took vacations to exotic places.

On the outside, her life looked idyllic. On the inside, it was not. Marital problems led to divorce. She left home with her four-year-old daughter. Later, she would get custody of her daughter. She would keep the house, and all the while she continued to work as a teacher.

Recovering and reinventing herself in the role of a working single mother was a big change for Mary. She sought help from the Episcopalian priest and the church community. Then, one day, a close friend introduced her to a tarot card reader who told her things no one could possibly have known. Mary felt consoled and hopeful. There was something to it all, she thought. For the first time, she felt she was receiving affirmation of a higher power — another "source" that she could tap into.

But *what* was this source? *Where* was it? *Who* was it? She became more curious. She took classes that taught any number of so-called "self-help" practices: positive thinking, visualization, meditation, self-hypnosis, repeating affirmations. She was told that she — like most people — was a "wounded warrior in need of healing." She was told she could have paranormal abilities, such as ESP; she could heal herself through past-life regression; and she could overcome fear with the help of healers. When negative thoughts entered her mind, she was told to say, "Cancel, cancel."

Some of it helped. Again, there always seemed to be some confirmation that a higher power was at work, enough confirmation to continue exploring. She taught about Native American culture and history in her classroom. Through that, she received a grant that allowed her to tour Navajo Indian reservations to learn about Native Americans and their education systems. Another time, at a Lakota reservation, she taught poverty-stricken children and learned more about Native American spiritual rituals, which intrigued her.

Once again, there was always something there — some sort of proof of the supernatural. She once took photos of a medicine man. When she developed the photographs, his image wasn't there. One time, Mary saw 12 eagles flying in a funnel and went to investigate. Turned out, the eagles were circling the gravesite of a Lakota Chief. How do you explain that? It was spectacular.

But something else was afoot. It seemed each new insight teetered on a thin line. On one side was light, on the other side was — what? Something else, whatever it was. She began having a recurring dream. In the dream, she would be walking in a long hallway lined with doors. She would go door to door and room to room, each containing some form of New Age practices in which she would participate. "But always at the end of the hallway, Jesus Christ was standing, looking at me," she said. "This dream happened so many times throughout the years, I know it vividly." You don't need a psychology degree to understand what He consciously was telling her: Keep walking the straight and narrow toward Christ, the Redeemer.

Nonetheless, in real life, Mary kept opening doors, and in each one, the light was growing progressively dimmer.

She attended seminars at top-dollar East Coast New Age institutes that offer a potpourri of courses. In one such institute, she took a shamanic class. She fell in with a self-described shaman who practiced his own form of Peruvian shamanism, had written several books, and had a following of fellow seekers. She was told of "soul-loss," which, in shamanic understanding, is a primary source of illness, depression, and mental confusion.

On one occasion, she was instructed to lie beside a man and, through meditation, journey into the "mythic" underworld to retrieve a "soul part" that was missing. This was called "soul retrieval." Afterwards, she told the man that during her meditation, she saw a distraught 12-year-old boy. Upon hearing this, the man broke down in tears. He shared with her that when he was 12, his mother left home with his sister to "go on a trip." They never returned. It was more confirmation for her that some spirit life, some mystical power, was afoot in the world.

She took more courses from the "shaman" on healing through "luminous energy fields" that supposedly surround the body. When he claimed he was a "shape shifter" and traveled out of his body as an animal — a cougar — between midnight and 4 a.m., Mary just had had about enough. Then, she learned he was sleeping with some of the women — the most vulnerable among them. It became clear he had a power over people, especially the women who were desperately looking to get "healed."

One night, following a conversation she had with another woman regarding their concerns, Mary had a nightmare in which she was confronted by a cougar. The next morning, the other woman said she had a similar dream. That's when Mary left the group.

Then, through a gathering of Native Americans in western Massachusetts, Mary met another man who led trips to Peru to partake in healing rituals with indigenous people in the jungles there. This man, too, called himself a shamanic healer. But he was different. He was a licensed and practicing psychologist who appeared to have a good, helping heart. He had developed an esoteric belief system that drew upon Peruvian Indian beliefs, Eastern religions, quasi-Christian, quasi-science, and New Age practices.

He claimed he could travel out of his body and perform long-distance healing. He taught that evil is self-created. He would teach how to tap into the powers of telepathy, and the group would practice it. He claimed people could ascend to invisible higher spheres and communicate with extraterrestrial beings that frequently travel in and out of Peru. He introduced his students to plant "spirit medicines" to aid in their healing. The students, including Mary, reported experiencing many "metaphysical changes."

She attended his seminars around the United States and joined him on tours to sacred sites in Peru, where she participated in native shamanic healing rituals. "It was all about healing yourself and others," Mary says.

Then, things started changing. She began to pick up on inconsistencies between words and actions. Secret and exclusive circles were being formed within the group. Punitive measures were drawn up for members of the group who were viewed as not toeing the line. "We started seeing immoral behavior, done without any conscience whatsoever," Mary says. Vulnerable, young women told Mary they had been duped into sexual encounters and then summarily discarded from that special relationship.

Eventually, everything had become very muddled for most of the people in the group. What was immoral was sold as "moral." What clearly had become destructive practices were sold as "helping and healing practices." And the mixing together of plant "spirit medicines" played a key role in the manipulations and the blurring of lines between reality and illusion.

Bad things happened. Really bad things.

Mary and others in the group felt this man sought to control what they were thinking. She was one of the first members of the original group to, as she says, "cast the devil out of my life." Something — some force, some *thing* — was very wrong, very dark. She left the group, but later she began to have nightmares. Many nightmares. In these nightmares, she was being dragged into the underworld where she could not escape. Distressed, she sought help from other New Age practitioners who confirmed that evil forces were targeting her, but these practitioners were completely helpless in their attempts to provide a remedy.

One night, she dreamed she was being sucked into quicksand. She awoke to the sound of her own voice screaming the words, "*Jesus! Mary! Joseph!*"

She jumped up and turned on all the lights. Her heart was pounding. What was happening? And where did *that* come from? *Jesus, Mary, and Joseph?*

She checked herself into an emergency room. The doctors declared she wasn't psychotic. She still believed this man who called himself a healer was somehow creating the images that were coming into her mind. After all, hadn't they practiced mental telepathy many times before? He didn't like that she had broken loose from his group. Then, she began having terrible dreams of loved ones being endangered and severely harmed.

One evening, she had visions — not dreams, but *visions* — of the man and Satan. "There was a presence in my room that was so evil, it made my skin crawl and my heart beat so fast and so hard that I thought it would come right through my chest," Mary says. "I could barely breathe or move. I was terrorized with fear." A voice told her she was engaged in a battle of good versus evil. In the vision, this healer man asked her, "Who is going to win this battle, Mary?"

He then told her she was going to experience the voices of hell that night. And she did. She tried praying the Our Father over and over again, but she couldn't get to the words "deliver us from evil." It was as if those words were blocked off from her.

By the next morning, she was back in the hospital. Her toes had severe lacerations, and she was in shock. She knows the wounds were self-inflicted. She can't explain it. She was later told by her spiritual director, a Catholic priest, that she had been attacked by "pure evil."

☦

"Let me just say that spiritual warfare is very real," says Mary in 2012, nearly seven years later. "It nearly cost me my life — my physical life and psychological well-being — a nightmare of nightmares that in my wildest imagination I never could have conceived. It also devastated my family and personal relationships."

She's speaking during a pilgrimage in 2012 to the National Shrine of The Divine Mercy in Stockbridge, Massachusetts. This is where, while strolling the grounds on her first visit a year prior, she came upon a welcome sight for weary eyes: The rays of the rising sun had formed an amazing interplay with the bronze statue of the Merciful Jesus, which greets visitors as they turn into the main parking plaza on Eden Hill. The rays seemed to stream from His Heart like the blood and water that gushed from His side at the crucifixion.

Dawn had just broken. It was Saturday, April 30, 2011, the kick-off of Divine Mercy Sunday Weekend. Even one of the Shrine volunteers who has been directing traffic for years each Divine Mercy Sunday Weekend had never seen anything like it. Mary pulled out her camera and clicked and clicked and clicked — 20-plus photos of what, for her, was a miracle.

"It was just so beautiful and miraculous," she recalls. "For me, it was a confirmation and a blessing."

A confirmation of what? That, after the decades she had spent wandering from spiritual movement to spiritual movement, she wound up back where she belongs. Through this beautiful moment at an early Saturday morning sunrise, she knew her sometimes harrowing search for meaning had come to an end, here at the feet of the risen Christ. She has found her spiritual home in the Divine Mercy. She has also understood very clearly that she needs to sound the alarm of danger about the multitude of cultish and occult healing practices, the panoply of spirituality without borders or without confining dogmas.

"Innumerable New Age 'healing techniques,' alternative therapies, Eastern philosophical thought, gurus, and shamanism are being marketed by major centers across the country," she says. "A lot of money was made then — and is still being made — and a lot of people have been tricked and hurt. There is no research, oversight, or accountability whatsoever about these programs. Anyone can declare themselves a healer." Indeed, even the medical profession has held forums on what to do about this problem. And in 2009, alarmed by the increasing popularity of New Age practices, the U.S. Conference of Catholic Bishops set specific guidelines as a response.

"During this time when I was enmeshed in it," says Mary, "I didn't believe the Devil really existed or that evil existed. That, by itself, I now know was extremely dangerous. You think your innocence protects you somehow, or that 'what you don't know, can't hurt you.' In retrospect, I walked into the Devil's nest. I now know that our spiritual hunger, our inner desire to find God, is what makes the New Age occult appeal to us. It diverts us from Him and into the underworld of spiritual confusion. It all seems benign at first. Even something as simple as a Ouija board opens the doors to Satan, and only Jesus Christ can close it."

Mary points to author Moira Noonan's book, *Ransomed from Darkness*, in which the author discusses her involvement as a New Age practitioner and her re-conversion to the Catholic Church. "In her analysis," Mary says, "she identifies the very real, demonic forces — Satanic forces — that I had faced. I wish I had known ahead of time, been told, been warned. My decisions might have been radically different. In retrospect, I now know that the Bible has countless warnings about these things." They include:

> Let no one be found among you who ... practices divination or sorcery, interprets omens, engages in witchcraft, or casts spells, or who is a medium or spiritist or who consults the dead. Anyone who does these things is detestable to the Lord (Dt 18:10-12).

> The coming of the lawless one will be in accordance with the work of Satan displayed in all kinds of counterfeit miracles, signs and wonders, and in every sort of evil that deceives those who are perishing. They perish because they refused to love the truth and so be saved (2 Thes 2:9-10).

Along with Scriptures' clear teaching against such practices, Mary learned that the New Age movement amounts to the return of a heresy that plagued the early Church. In his book *Crossing the Threshold of Hope*, Pope John Paul II writes of this ancient heresy known as Gnosticism and its connection with the New Age:

> A separate issue is the return of ancient Gnostic ideas under the guise of the so-called *New Age*. We cannot delude ourselves that this will lead toward a renewal of religion. It is only a new way of practicing Gnosticism — that attitude of the spirit that, in the name of a profound knowledge of God,

results in distorting His Word and replacing it with purely human words. Gnosticism never completely abandoned the realm of Christianity. Instead, it has always existed side by side with Christianity, sometimes taking the shape of a philosophical movement, but more often assuming the characteristics of a religion or a para-religion in distinct, if not declared, conflict with all that is essentially Christian.

In 2011, before she learned about the message of Divine Mercy and St. Faustina, Mary's primary care physician introduced her to the Massachusetts-based, Catholic Church-sanctioned healing ministry of Frank Kelly. His near-death experience following an electrocution led him to become a strong advocate of the Sacraments of the Church and the Rosary. A Jesuit priest is his spiritual director. "Life changed in a major way for me," Mary says. "Frank told me to say, 'Jesus, come into my heart,' and then he prayed over me. After I met Frank and heard his story and his practical, *real-life* Catholicism with its real-life mysticism, I knew in my heart that this is what I had been searching for.

"I began attending his gatherings. I experienced an overwhelming peace that I had never known before. Unlike people in the New Age movement that I've encountered, Frank would never say that *he* was the healer. Only God heals. As he says so often, 'It's not *me* — I can't heal an ant!'"

Mary says that through Frank, God brought her fully back to the "true Catholic Church. Almost immediately, some of my bad habits that I had attempted to extinguish for many years, such as numbing my emotional pain through drinking alcohol, disappeared. Then, in a very devoted and heartfelt way, I began to pray the Rosary daily and attend daily Mass and receive Holy Communion. I was so thankful for this moment in my life, so grateful to God for this deep inner peace of divine love and mercy and grace."

Mary was surprised at what she found in the Church. There was mysticism she had never known about and mercy like she had never imagined. After a difficult journey back, the heartbreak she now feels is for others who have been, and still are being, similarly misled. "In retrospect, as a teenager, I could only see and understand that the Church was all about rules, sternness, and punishment, and that stayed with me throughout my life," Mary says.

In 2011, she learned of the Divine Mercy message and devotion after she joined in her physician's yearly pilgrimage to Lourdes, France, and other holy sites. In Lourdes, she was introduced to the Chaplet of the Divine Mercy by two sisters from Florida. When the sisters found out that Mary lived near Boston, Massachusetts — about a three-hour drive from the National Shrine of The Divine Mercy — they encouraged her to visit. "I didn't know anything about the Shrine," Mary said. "I put it on my agenda."

Surely, it was God's Providence that led her to the Shrine on Divine Mercy Sunday Weekend. Surely, it was His Providence that she saw the rays of the Divine Mercy.

She says, "We all know there is a mind-body-spirit connection. But it's not all about 'me, myself, and I' self-empowerment and 'alignment with the Universe.' And it's not all about the 'We are the ones we have been waiting for' sort of talk that we so often hear. Rather, it's about a loving God who, through Jesus Christ, gives us the true gifts of His love, His mercy, His blessings, and His grace.

"Divine Mercy Sunday Weekend at the Shrine was full of very tenderhearted blessings of this mystic nature, too many to name. Gratefully, I now pray the Divine Mercy Chaplet while looking at these photographs of the Divine Mercy rays of Christ. For me, these photographs represent how much our loving and kind God shines His light upon us and calls us back to Himself.

"After 40 years of seeking," says Mary, "all my experiences — the deceivingly good, the bad, and the very ugly — have taught me one thing about these present, precious moments in my life, and that is: You know you know, when you have the real peace of God."

Mary has come back home.

Felix Carroll

CHAPTER 15

Dr. Scot Bateman

Redefining the Term 'Good Doctor'

At that moment, I saw the Lord Jesus, His eyes filled with tears, and He said to me, "You see, My daughter, what great compassion I have for [suffering children]. Know that it is they who uphold the world."

— Diary of St. Faustina, 286

Dr. Scot Bateman walks down a hallway lined with doors. Through some of the doors, children are recovering. Through others, children are dying. Family members, looking worn and rattled, can be seen at bedsides. Through the pressure of illness and the heat of emotion, it's as if their whole worlds have condensed and crystallized to the size of a hospital room. This is their encampment. For some, this is their nightmare.

At the nurses' station, a medical team talks in hushed tones while examining an X-ray. In the hallway, everyone — even the maintenance staff — walks as if on padded paws, as if in a sacred space. Which they are. Dr. Bateman makes his way through a door, then through another door, then down a hallway, and into his office at the University of Massachusetts Memorial Children's Medical Center's Pediatric Critical Care Unit, for which he serves as chief.

A big window overlooks the city streets of Worcester, Massachusetts. In comparison to sick children, everything below seems trifling or not real. How does he do this for a living? He smiles — a half smile, really. "I tried to talk myself out of it many times, and I can't," he says. Dr. Bateman, a convert to Catholicism, is a member of Healthcare Professionals for Divine Mercy, an apostolate of the Marian Fathers of the Immaculate Conception. That explains a lot. He draws his strength from his faith. He encourages his patients to do likewise, whatever their religion may be.

"Spirituality is an essential component in the pediatric critical care unit," he says. "For the patients, for the parents, and for the medical staff, too, unless you have a way of dealing with suffering, you can't be here."

For as long as he can remember, Dr. Bateman wanted to be a doctor. Growing up in Lake Tahoe, California, anytime his classmates were injured in the playground, he could be counted on to rush to their aid. He'd tell them he could help because he planned to be a doctor when he grew up.

His spiritual life was less certain. His mother was a Christian Scientist, his father a Lutheran. He recalls attending church services maybe five times at the most during his childhood. He knew he wanted to be a doctor. He knew he wanted to help people. But he didn't consider the role of God in his life and in his work until one day in 1998, while he was serving as a second-year resident at Children's Hospital in Boston.

He was making his rounds and came to the bedside of a terminally ill 11-year-old girl named Emily. She had T-cell lymphoma and was admitted as a last-ditch effort. Every day, he'd tell her a joke (such as "Why do gorillas have big nostrils? Because they have big fingers.") He recalls her laughter. It was hearty, genuine, and infectious. She imbued innocence. She radiated trust and hope, even as her body became ravaged with tumors.

She asked him through knowing tears, "It's not good, is it?" "No, it's not," he responded. She contemplated that answer. Then, she suddenly asked, "Scot, what is it going to feel like when I die?"

That question stretched beyond his preconceived notions of doctoring. No one taught him how to answer that in medical school. He recalls thinking how words such as "*You can fight*," or "*Be strong*," or "*Hold on*" came to mind, but they rang hollow. She demanded honesty. She knew she was dying. "I think you will probably feel like you are falling deeper and deeper asleep," he told her, his voice quivering. "You will find it harder and harder to wake up and see all of us here. But finally you won't be able to wake up. Instead, you will be in your dreams from then on."

The words hung in the air. She stared at him directly. Then, she finally said, "I like my dreams." She started crying uncontrollably, but with a sense of relief and peace — not fear.

"And I saw just grace — grace like I had never experienced, pure and simple," Dr. Bateman recalls, describing this child who would soon die. In her last remaining days, she slipped in and out of consciousness. She said goodbye to family and friends. Wearily, she would ask Scot for a joke. He would oblige. At one point, she motioned for him to come closer. She whispered, "Scot, you are going to be a great doctor."

At the time, he would not have called his choice of careers as one guided by faith. Now he does. "I have found that you cannot be around suffering too long before you want to try to understand it," he says. "You can't see an innocent child on a ventilator, severely injured or sick, and not question why they are suffering." This search for meaning forced him to confront a question he wasn't prepared for. He was speaking with a fellow physician, Ann, a Catholic, about a patient who had died. Ann asked him, "Where is God in your life?" He wasn't prepared for the question, and he didn't have a pat answer.

"Ann's question, and my lack of a sound answer, made it clear that deep inside me was some sense of faith, trust, and belief, even though I had no substantial religious background," Dr. Bateman says.

"I could not name these feelings. I had no vocabulary with which to have a conversation about them. I was completely unable to articulate what I had felt inside of me.

"But I recognized that some guiding force had been calling me throughout my life and my practice and had played a major role in my decisions. I guess the Holy Spirit was finally saying, 'I have been right here, just get to know Me better.'"

He "church-shopped," which confirmed for him that all the major faiths in the world are looking for the same thing: meaning found only in a merciful Creator. He felt drawn to the Catholic Church, above all. For in it, with its traditions and Sacraments, he found a sacredness he had experienced only within the confines of a pediatric intensive care unit.

In 2002, he attended a physicians' conference in Atlanta, Georgia, when he felt drawn to step inside Sacred Heart Church, near where he was staying. It was the feast of Pentecost, the day the Church celebrates the descent of the Holy Spirit upon the Blessed Virgin Mary and the 12 apostles. It's also considered the "birthday of the Church." Dr. Bateman had no idea what Pentecost was.

But inside the church that morning, he experienced a Pentecost of his own. He felt a call to receive Holy Communion even though he had not yet been received into the Church. He had no clue that receiving Communion in his case was forbidden. Still, he followed the line up to the altar. He ate the Body. He drank the Blood. Then, he says, "When I went back to my pew, an indescribable sense of warmth flowed through me. It began in the pit of my stomach and spread to my limbs, to the pews, to the people around me, to the stained-glass windows, to the bricks, to the mortar, I was in communion with everything around me. I began to weep uncontrollably because of an intense combination of unworthiness and awe at the existence of God and love.

"When I stopped crying, the church was empty, and the Mass was over. Then, I began to laugh just as uncontrollably as I had wept, knowing that nobody would ever believe what had just happened to me. I felt a profound sense of sadness because of all that I had not known for all of those years, as well as a sense of joy for the beauty, the feeling of peace, and the understanding of truth that had come over me."

Along with the grace of spiritual awareness, came rejection. At that time, his marriage was collapsing. He and his wife had a two-year-old and a four-year-old. One day, while lying on his office floor, he felt compelled to stand up and head straight down to St. Ignatius Church. There, he got down on his knees and asked God how such a beautiful journey to Him could be wracked with so much personal pain.

"I closed my eyes and said out loud, 'Well, God, it's in Your hands. I'm done.'" He recalls that at that moment the organ sounded, and standing before him was a colleague of his from Children's Hospital in Boston, who then introduced him to the director of religious education.

He soon entered the Rite of Christian Initiation for Adults (RCIA) and was received into the Church on the Easter Vigil in 2004. Meanwhile, his marriage ended. He spent the next two years living alone in a small apartment close to his two children. "I was alone and broken from the divorce," he says. "This was the darkest time of my life. But it was also a time of incredible spiritual growth, deflating my pride, leading me to spend a great deal of time in prayer and reading poetry. I was also drawn to read conversion stories, like the story of St. Paul. They are a testament to the power and the mystery of God." He took Luke as his Confirmation name because Luke was both a convert and a physician.

He maintains a great relationship with his ex-wife. He is raising his two children as Catholics. He has since remarried a Catholic physician, and they have a child together.

Through it all, that 11-year-old girl, Emily, had altered and expanded forever what Dr. Bateman calls his once "feeble" definition of a good doctor. Being a good doctor, he now says, means being a merciful presence at the bedside of the sick and dying.

Day to day, Dr. Bateman and his staff work in the trenches, ministering — medically and spiritually — to families undergoing what he calls "the worst nightmare of their lives." They witness anger and fear and extreme stress. They hear yelling, screaming, crying.

They also hear laughter, and they often witness something beautiful. "We see people at their best, even when circumstances are at their worst." They are witnesses to love — the unconditional kind. The kind that's both intimate and universal, that connects with a Higher Power. The kind that points to the God of mercy.

The Pediatric Critical Care Unit at UMass Memorial treats more than 700 patients annually, from newborns to 18-year-olds. Dr. Bateman has trained his staff to look for opportunities to speak with parents and family members about how they are doing. "What we've experienced is that you only have to scratch at the surface and it comes out: Spirituality is usually right there no matter what religion you are. I've realized that, whoever we are, we're all searching for the same things: faith, hope, and love."

✝

During his conversion, Dr. Bateman saw an image of Michelangelo's Pieta, and it resonated powerfully for him. In it, an anguished Mary holds the broken Body of her Son after He is lowered down from the cross. In the pediatric ICU, Dr. Batemen sees parents undergoing a similar grief to Mary's — holding their own dying children till their last breath, until it's time to let go. For instance, he watches a little 10-year-old boy with a severe head injury on mechanical ventilation with his arms outstretched and lines running into his veins, and he sees the image of Christ on the cross. The crucifix has taken on new meaning for him as a result. "I now see love when I see the crucifix. I appreciate how love is present even in the face of catastrophe and heartbreak."

Interestingly, while it was the Sacred Heart image in Sacred Heart Church that first sparked Dr. Bateman's conversion, it was the image of the Divine Mercy that defined for him what Jesus was all about — what He wished to give and what He wished to receive in return. In the image, Jesus is stepping forward, making the first move to give the gift of His mercy. "We love, because He first loved us," says the apostle John (1 Jn 4:19).

"The Divine Mercy image shares a message that's so applicable in healthcare delivery — that image of sharing, Jesus sharing His light, sharing His love in a very active way," says Dr. Bateman. "You can almost feel it come on you when you see it. It's what we do in healthcare. That's the image we try to project."

Dr. Bateman says he has learned from the message of the Divine Mercy how much Christ loves us and wants us to trust in Him and to love others as He loves us. "Being able to be an instrument of mercy for meek children and their families — I view that as a privilege," he says. A privilege because in a sick child — in their meekness, their dignity, their love, their trust, their suffering — he sees Christ's image. "It's like when you look at the crucifix," he says, "you see both pain and beauty. If you don't see both, you're not getting it. Appreciating both as real is what opens up the sense of the divine."

His staff feels free to ask families if they need a member of the clergy. They are careful to give patients and their families quiet space. They treat the Pediatric Intensive Care Unit as a sacred place. They don't specifically engage in religious ritual, but there's a palpable atmosphere there of prayerfulness. They make it known that, while they are highly trained medical professionals, they are not single-minded. They are human. Like medical schools throughout the country, Dr. Bateman now assimilates spiritual care into training, recognizing connections between medical and spiritual interventions.

"What I'm trying to do is to incorporate the big-picture stuff earlier in our training for our residents and institutes. No one ever did that for me," says Dr. Batemen, who received a fellowship on clinical pastoral education for healthcare providers. "The idea is to bring the topic academically to the forefront so that we are thinking about it — about how contemplative practices can lead to the divine and about how there's a great need to incorporate the divine into how we interact with patients and families. Solid research tells us that a family's ability to cope with a child's death is related to their belief in the transcendence of the parent-child relationship. If we know a child's survival is out of the question, then we hope that we can help a family come to terms with its loss. This realization is something that I did not appreciate early in my career."

Medical students and members of his staff are thankful to have such training. With illness and tragedy all around them, his staff also, privately, at times breaks down in tears themselves. How could they not? Children represent their parents' hopes and dreams. And sometimes hopes and dreams shatter.

As for tears shed for suffering children, Christ Himself sheds them, too. At one point in her *Diary*, St. Faustina implores Jesus to look upon the tears of suffering little children. She writes: "At that moment, I saw the Lord Jesus, His eyes filled with tears, and He said to me, 'You see, My daughter, what great compassion I have for them. Know that it is they who uphold the world'" (286).

"If the sight of suffering children didn't affect us," says Dr. Bateman, "We'd be in the wrong field. As soon as it gets easier, I'm in the wrong field." Emotional burnout stands as the great job hazard. But there's a flip side: the joy of seeing kids get better. "It fuels hope," says Dr. Bateman, "which is essential to working here."

He does this work because, he says, a sick child deserves everything — the best medical care and the best spiritual care. He does this because every child has an undying, beautiful spirit, and that spirit is a source of strength.

He recalls how the famous medical missionary Dr. Ted Kuhn said, "Years ago, I was challenged to ask God to break my heart with the things that break His heart." It's one of Dr. Bateman's favorite quotes. He still remembers Emily, that 11-year-old girl. To this day, her memory can make his eyes well up. But her memory, he says, also "enlivens each day with hope, giving me the courage to smile."

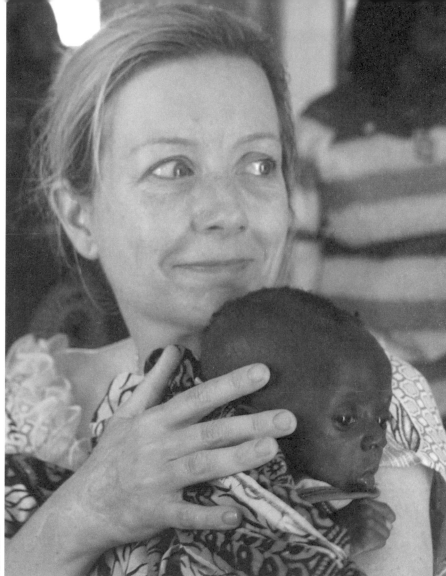

CHAPTER 16

Kellie Ross

Mercy Is a Verb

Jesus to St. Faustina:

I demand from you deeds of mercy, which are to arise out of love for Me. You are to show mercy to your neighbors always and everywhere.

— Diary of St Faustina, 742

There are no pinks and baby blues here. No celebratory cigars. No balloons. Just the moans and screams of women giving birth. In this maternity ward, a beautiful boy has just been born. Now he's dying.

"Where is his mother?" asks Kellie Ross. Someone points down the hall where a woman is shrieking and hitting herself on the head and chest. She's being stitched up, without anesthesia — because there is none. Moments later, Kellie passes other women who are agonizing in labor. There are no labor rooms, not even sheets. Women are simply walking back and forth or holding onto chairs for support until it's time to deliver.

The equipment is ancient. "It's two generations old," says Dr. Scott Ross, Kellie's husband and a family practitioner. There is one doctor for the entire hospital, and amidst rushing around tending to patients, the doctor finds a moment to make it known to Kellie — hopefully, to the world — that he needs help, money, equipment, support of some kind, any kind, something.

He needs prayers.

In the pediatric unit, a baby is anemic. Other babies in the same room suffer from infection and malnourishment. Farther down the corridor, a newborn girl is crying, screaming, pleading. She's in her mother's arms. Her mother sits motionless. Maybe stoic. Maybe numb from grief. The mother hands Kellie the baby, whom she takes into her arms.

"She's dying," Kellie says, tears welling up as she rocks the baby and coos. "This baby is dying." The baby is literally starving to death. A nurse explains that the mother cannot produce milk to feed the child, the mother has no money for food, and the hospital doesn't have any baby formula.

Back on the bus, everyone looks shell-shocked.

"We need to pray the Chaplet of Divine Mercy for the children of Cote d'Ivoire," says Kellie, director of the Missionaries of Our Lady of Divine Mercy, a Virginia-based Catholic mission that has come to this West African nation to bring material and spiritual assistance. The Missionaries begin solemn prayer as the bus turns back onto a two-lane road toward their next sorrowful stop.

... For the sake of His sorrowful Passion, have mercy on us and on the whole world. ...

☦

Two months before this mission in 2009, standing beside a row of clothes racks inside the House of Mercy in Manassas, Virginia, a center that serves the poor, Kellie Ross is explaining her goal in life: to get to heaven and to bring as many people with her as she can.

"I spent half my life offending God," she says. "In the second half of my life, Divine Mercy is my ministry in reparation."

A native of Washington State, Kellie describes her younger years as "out of control and miserable." She made "many bad choices." And when she hit rock bottom, she was alone and destitute and only days away from having to move into a homeless shelter.

Then, she received a letter in the mail offering her substantial financial assistance to return to college. It was a miracle. She earned a bachelor's degree in international studies in 1990. She knew she had compassion for people. This was always the case. Even in grammar school if a classmate would get injured, Kellie would feel the pain. One way or another, she knew she would have to put her compassion to action, and that's what led her to eventually earn her degree in nursing. While taking care of the sick and dying as a nurse in the intermediate care unit at Fairfax Hospital in Virginia, Kellie realized something was missing. What was it? God — that's what. Without God in her life, she knew she would be unable to make sense of the suffering in the world — her own suffering and the suffering of those around her.

"I realized how much I needed faith," she said.

All through her teens and early twenties, she had searched for truth, for meaning, for goodness and beauty, but in all the wrong places: namely, in a lifestyle built upon self-gratification rather than self-sacrifice.

She finally found God — realizing that there is a God, and that He doesn't point fingers — when she was in her late twenties. It was in 2005. She was married by then. She and Scott had a date night, the first since the birth of their two young boys. They wouldn't be going to a restaurant. They wouldn't be going to the movies. Instead, she told Scott she felt called to go to Holy Mass, an odd choice for a night out considering she wasn't a churchgoer. But Scott figured, "Hey, if that's what she wants to do, let's do it."

It was the feast of the Sacred Heart. They were in All Saints Church in Manassas. The priest's words during the homily pierced her soul. He said: "Are you lonely? Are you tired? Do you feel like God has abandoned you? Is your marriage flat? Do you struggle with your children? Do you worry about finances?" Then, he paused and leaned over the pulpit and said, "I promise you, I promise you, if you enthrone Jesus in your home, you will have peace in your family, you will have peace in your marriage, you will have peace with your children. You will have no worries. I promise you.'"

After Mass, she and Scott stuck around for the Holy Hour. When the priest brought out the monstrance, she turned to Scott and said, "What is that? And why is my heart calling for that?"

"You've never seen a monstrance?" Scott asked.

"At that moment, that one moment, watching the monstrance changed my life," says Kellie. "I recognized what my soul had been looking for all these years. I didn't know about the Eucharist. I didn't know about the Real Presence of Jesus in the Eucharist. Nothing."

She knelt before the monstrance and wept inconsolably. She felt called to greater service. Soon after, she was home leafing through a copy of *Marian Helper* magazine, when an article entitled "One Million Times Greater" caught her attention. It discussed ways people can help spread the message of Divine Mercy. The article included an image of the Divine Mercy with a magnifying glass over the Heart of Jesus. That image summarized for Kellie what she felt called to do. She wanted to magnify the Lord's mercy, so that others who were lost or lonely or in spiritual and financial crisis would come to know that Jesus is real and that He calls us to a deep, personal relationship with Himself.

Kellie went to a talk hosted by a local church. She doesn't remember the talk, but she does remember going to confession and meeting Fr. Jack Fullen, a retired priest, in the confessional. She had the copy of *Marian Helper* magazine with her. She had been praying about starting a Divine Mercy cenacle or prayer group in her parish, Holy Trinity in Bristow, Virginia. At the end of the confession, she asked Fr. Jack if he would be willing to be the cenacle's spiritual director. He said he would love to.

"As I was getting up to walk out of confession, he grabbed my arm and stopped me and said, 'Do you smell that?'" Kellie recalls. All the sudden, the room was filled with the smell of roses, and there were no roses in sight.

"You smell the roses?" Fr. Jack asked. He said, "I think God has big plans for us."

✝

From the outset, this was their charism or call: to see mercy as a verb — that is, a word that describes an action to be taken. The action to be taken was to first form a Eucharistic Apostles of The Divine Mercy cenacle or prayer group. It was just five people, plus Fr. Jack, all sitting around a card table reading and discussing the *Diary of St. Faustina*, learning to live the message of Divine Mercy through the cenacle formation program, which is based on Scripture, the *Catechism of the Catholic Church*, and the *Diary*, and then to turn to the Sacraments, particularly the Sacrament of Reconciliation.

The number of cenacle members doubled, then tripled, then quadrupled until it was time to take more action. They decided to live the message of Divine Mercy through helping those in need — the poor, the abused, the forgotten. When the number of people in critical need exceeded their expectations, it was time to take further action. They formed Missionaries of Our Lady of Divine Mercy, and on November 1, 2006, All Saints Day, they opened up the House of Mercy. Everything would be given away for free as a testimony to their trust in God.

The 2,000-square-foot House of Mercy looks like a thrift shop — sort of. What distinguishes it are several things. The dangling paper rectangles attached to the clothing are not price tags but prayercards. The House of Mercy includes a well-stocked Catholic library. There are classrooms for spiritual instruction. Through private donations and grants, the House of Mercy serves the spiritual and material needs of all who come knocking at the door. It gives away new shoes, beds, and school supplies. It gives away "gently used" clothing. It provides financial assistance for funerals, medication, and pre-natal care. The House of Mercy has volunteers from area Catholic churches who help support the programs the ministry offers. Father Francis Peffley, pastor of Holy Trinity Parish in Gainesville, serves as spiritual director.

All along the way, Kellie says she believes God speaks to her through the *Diary of St. Faustina*, which documents St. Faustina's revelations in the 1930s that have sparked the modern Divine Mercy movement.

She says, "I remember reading *Diary* entry 742 where Jesus says, 'I demand from you deeds of mercy, which are to arise out of love for Me. You are to show mercy to your neighbors always and everywhere. You must not shrink from this or try to excuse or absolve yourself from it.' I thought, 'Wow, He *demands* it. It's not a request. He *demands* deeds of mercy, and there are no excuses."

Men and women are going hungry in D.C.? No excuses. As part of their ministry, the Missionaries pack up food, clothing, prayercards, and sacramentals, and then they distribute them to the poor in D.C.

Children in northern Virginia are without clothes and food and school supplies? No excuses.

People are living without seeking God, and their souls are in jeopardy? No excuses.

"We have to help," says Kellie. "We cannot keep living under the assumption that other people will help."

Back to the word "action." If this were for a movie, the director would have yelled, "Cut!" by now. But here we are, Monday, June 15, 2009, in the battered and bombed-out city of Bouake (rhymes with Milwaukee) in northernmost Cote d'Ivoire. Why West Africa? Because children have been orphaned. Because 40 percent of the infrastructure of this country was destroyed by the civil war that lasted from 2002-2007. Because there's no money here, no foreign investment, little medical care, little food, little hope. And because Jesus told St. Faustina, "I demand from you deeds of mercy. ... You must not shrink from this."

His Excellency Marie-Daniel Dadiet, Archbishop of Korhogo, asked for help. During a trip to the United States, the Archbishop paid a visit to the House of Mercy. He and Kellie stepped out to have tea at a nearby McDonald's. Sitting across from Kellie, the Archbishop leaned in and asked her, "Will you help my people? They are suffering."

Some people in her community have wondered, "Why help Africa? The needs are so great here." The only sense Kellie herself can make of it is this: "Because they've asked, because there's a need, and because, with the grace of God, we can."

Mercy is a verb. No excuses.

✝

In Bouake, Kellie and the 10 other Missionaries on the trip are in an orphanage. Cries ricochet off the concrete floors. Forty children, from newborns to teens, are stuffed inside a space the size of a doublewide mobile home. Practically no natural light streams in. And not a single toy can be seen. Children wearing rags meet us at the gate. Some aren't shy. They wish to touch the visitors as if to see if we are real. They wish to hug us. And so they do, freely. The local parish, with the help of several women who barely have the means to care for themselves, are doing their best to keep the children safe and alive. The women are sitting cross-legged on the bare floor feeding babies a mixture of rice and goats' milk.

The Missionaries are being led around town by Fr. George Hoka, vicar general of the Archdiocese of Bouake. "We have so many needs," he says. "We need everything." He wipes his forehead with his sleeve.

Here in this orphanage, they need food, clothing, more space, and more warm adult bodies to provide care and love. Kellie and her group know their limitations, and it's heartbreaking and difficult to accept — knowing the needs here are far greater than they expected, far greater than their ministry can fulfill. In the orphanage, they steal silent, mournful glances at each other. They do know that when they get back home, they will shake the trees and ask all those who support their work in northern Virginia to also support sending aid here. They also know they can pray. They know they can hand out images of Jesus, the Divine Mercy, and they do.

There's only so much a small group can do.

They will pray because they have all come to know that prayer works.

Scott Ross wanders around the orphanage doing quick assessments. "That baby there is probably two months old," he says, pointing to a crib. "She's not growing. She's refluxing severely."

One boy is so impoverished he is wearing a girl's dress. The orphanage hasn't the funds to buy him clothing for a boy.

The Missionaries are told the backgrounds of some of the children — short in details, long in suffering. This boy here, his father was killed in the war. His father's family then came and confiscated everything worth anything, leaving this boy and his siblings and their mother homeless and penniless. The boy was brought here. No one knows where the other children are or where the mother is. They don't know much except that this boy likes to plant his feet on the ground, jump straight up in the air, and then crash land with a mischievous and contagious laugh. The boy wants to fly.

And this girl was found in the street, on her back, nearly dead. And this boy's mother died during childbirth. No one knows the whereabouts of his father. The boy is three years old.

He's wearing only a T-shirt — a hand-me-down with an image of the cartoon character Dora the Explorer, a T-shirt that indicates that someone somewhere in the Western world has made an effort to help. Someone has sent clothes. But any past humanitarian efforts aimed at Cote d'Ivoire have trickled down to nearly nothing.

Kellie presents the children with a Frisbee. But she knows it's a band-aid on a hemorrhage. The brokenness here is so severe it can only be reassembled through the mortar of Christ's mercy — and sustained attention. The Missionaries hand out prayercards. Again, as with everywhere they go, the prayercards are received like proverbial manna.

Interestingly, perhaps miraculously, as the Missionaries entered a tiled breezeway into the orphanage, past the lines of tiny shirts and pants and underwear drying on a series of cords, they are startled to see that Divine Mercy has preceded them. Old and weather-worn images of the Divine Mercy are plastered onto the battered walls. Kellie is relieved. It's a sign, right? It has to be a sign. Jesus is present here.

From the orphanage, Kellie and the Missionaries travel along a winding road to a hospital. But calling it a hospital seems generous. It's a walled off compound where the mentally ill are quarantined. The place is filthy.

A man with disfigured legs crawls across the floor like a crab. Bodies that have no reason to get up, stay down. But some of the patients are assembled as the group arrives. They sing a song for the Missionaries, a tribal song, a folk song. It's a brave attempt at joy. But clearly there is little joy here. Inside a bunkhouse, there are no bunks, only blankets on hard floors and flies buzzing around. A garden hose snakes across the brown earth. It leads to a toilet and more flies. The hose is covered with what look like rubber strips from a bicycle inner tube that have been tied tight like tourniquets to stem the leaks. Maybe the patches work, and maybe they don't. There's no way of knowing because when you turn the spigot, no water comes out anyway — just a cough of air, like a last gasp.

Back outside, Kellie wants to be introduced to a young boy. He has a beautiful face. He's eight years old. He is completely out of place here among the older, clearly sick, patients. His ailment? Epilepsy, a common chronic neurological disorder that can be easily treated with the right medication. But here in Cote d'Ivoire, there are no medications available for epilepsy — or if the medications do exist, most people cannot afford them. That means that this eight-year-old boy's epilepsy is cause for him to be kept quarantined with the mentally ill in dark rooms, on hard floors, surrounded by bare walls, and amidst the horror of screams and wails and whimpers, and the stagnant smell of decay.

Kellie is hugging him. She then bends down upon her knees and kisses the spot where his left hand used to be. His left hand is burnt down to the nub. Kellie learns that during a seizure recently, he fell into a fire. His other hand and arm were also disfigured from the incident.

The boy is so clearly out of place here. He's a boy you'd see at your kids' elementary school. A boy with a shy smile. The girls would love him. Kellie and Scott's sons, Jake and Sam, are along on the mission. They go back into the bus and return with a gift for the boy. It's a ball, probably the first toy he's ever owned, another band-aid on a hemorrhage. Jake and Sam have given the boy a ball, but the boy has clearly given an even greater gift to them.

Earlier, Sam, in particular, was having a difficult time with the heat and with hunger. Such discomforts were new to him. Now, in a powerful moment, this boy with epilepsy has drawn Sam out of himself. Kellie would later remark how heartening it was to see her son turn from his own troubles in order to focus on the suffering of another. "A ball was exchanged, but more importantly, a gift of Divine Mercy was exchanged," she would later say.

Kellie watches as the eight-year-old boy is led back within the walls of a hospital he doesn't belong in, another child in Cote d'Ivoire walking a long and lonely road to Calvary.

"Kellie physically feels the suffering of others," says Fr. Jack. "She's always had a deep compassion to relieve the misery of others, and that's what drives her. She wants to serve the poor. She has a real gift to serve the poor."

He's speaking from the back of the bus that the Missionaries have been lent for the journey. It's a journey of prayer for a country in great need of mercy. The Missionaries are giving talks in standing-room-only parish churches. They're now on a bumpy road heading out of the city of Abidjan to the nation's capital of Yamoussoukro three hours away.

The bus passes a military checkpoint on a pockmarked road. It's a rest area of sorts, covered in litter and smelling of diesel. Young women sell mangos and cocoa beans, and heavily armed government soldiers with stone-cold expressions keep traffic in check with heavy strips of steel spikes that they roll in front of each vehicle. Two soldiers climb aboard the bus and walk up and down the aisle saying nothing. Then, they disembark and wave the bus on.

"How can anyone say India is poorer than this?" Kellie asks.

The trash is nearly everywhere. Nearly any place with people, there's trash: in the rivers, the streets, beside the mud huts in the north and the shantytowns down south. We snap photos of the trash as we pass through squalor-filled streets. We take photos of it, because none of us have ever seen anything like it. As we wend our way up and down the heart of Cote d'Ivoire, our indignation about nonchalant littering recedes by slow degrees because we realize there is no trash pick-up here. There are no trash bins. To place the trash we generate on the bus into a bag to be deposited later is to engage in an exercise of futility because there will be no place anyway, no matter where we go, to deposit that bag.

The trash is the mark of the systemic collapse of the social order here due to prolonged poverty and civil war. You can't drink the water. You can't swim in the once-beautiful lakes and rivers of a nation that 20 years ago was preparing its southern beaches to become a tourist mecca. In 2006, more than 100,000 Ivorians had to seek medical treatment after being poisoned as a result of toxic waste dumped in Abidjan. You can't walk arm and arm down the street with your loved one without navigating through mounds of garbage.

Witnessing it from a caravan whose passengers have traveled 7,000 miles from home seeking to save souls, you cannot help but to view all this garbage as a symptom of something else, of sin without fear of consequences. We are wallowing in it, drowning in it, killing ourselves through it. But there's a refuge from all this trash. We've seen it. It's not mere coincidence that the only places we've seen that are swept clean, the only places with garbage cans, the only places kept tidy are the grounds of the Catholic churches here. When all goes quiet again after Holy Mass, you can hear it: the *pfft, pfft, pfft* of brooms, the assertion of order.

The priests we meet all over this country invariably are praying for not only peace but peace and *order.* They pray for political stability, so people in their land can resume the pursuit of their dreams. But they know all this talk of peace and order is meaningless without first building a foundation of faith.

"The reason you have no order," Kellie says, as we enter the nation's capital of Yamoussoukro, "is because you have no 'order.'" By that, she means that only through religious formation, through a contemplative life that helps nourish and guide our actions, can we build true community, where people put God above all things and seek to serve God by serving His people who are in greatest need. Christ gave Himself on the cross for all of us. He wants us to see Him in the least among us.

From the bus, we see the trash, and it seems so incongruous with the yearnings of these people, the smiling people who clearly want something better, the people who reach out to receive the Divine Mercy prayercards the Missionaries pass out. They take the prayercards and clutch them to their chests. As the Missionaries wend their way northward, as the land turns from tropical to savannah, they are a welcome spectacle. A bus carrying Caucasians is not common here in Cote d'Ivoire, a country in which Western tourists are warned against visiting due to the unrest. People wave and smile and tug on each other when they see us. They look, they point, they wave.

These people yearn for something else. Many of their schools were destroyed during the civil war from 2002-2007. Eighty percent of Ivorians live below the poverty line. Many children were left orphaned or severely injured. Many children don't attend schools because there is neither money for schools nor teachers.

They're a people sorely disillusioned by false promises and false starts. In Yamoussoukro, we suddenly emerge from a two-lane road into five-lane-wide thoroughfares that are nearly devoid of traffic, roads built with expectations that never materialized. Busses and billboards advertise a lifestyle few people can afford, selling hair gels, cell phone plans, sofas, and, perhaps most disturbing, a skin cream called "Glow White" with a seductive-looking Caucasian woman. The side roads are paved, too, but tracked with mud from the bush because, despite the dreams of building a shining capital and a modern economy, most of the citizens here still survive through anything they can salvage from the land: lumber ribbed with fresh hatchet marks, mangoes, bananas, homemade charcoal, and thatch for roofs. Many people go barefoot. Many wear T-shirts that bear the cultural markings of the West — of Penn State, of Raleigh Parks and Rec Dept., of a Las Vegas slot machine, of Sponge Bob Square Pants — heaved from humanitarian efforts, the markings must seem like hieroglyphics to most Ivorians.

And amidst it all, in the streets, are the beautiful children. It's difficult to fathom the origin of a business plan in which countless children sell small packets of tissues for the equivalent of three pennies in nearly every large town. And where do they get these tissues, anyway? Whatever the case may be, like the people in this Divine Mercy caravan, these children see promise in bringing comfort to a country on the verge of tears.

We wave to them, and they smile and wave back and say sweet things to us in French. Then, they skip off together, a blessing of tiny tissue tycoons, waving and tugging on each other and skipping away, through the trash.

In the shadow of a parliament building under construction, on a barren stretch of five-lane thoroughfare, a peasant woman with a clutch of twigs from a palm tree is bended upon one knee.

She's sweeping debris into a pile.

A pile that's a prayer.

A prayer for order.

✝

It's drizzling. People on the roadside huddle under simple shelters with roofs made of thatch. Some shelters have walls. Others do not. The bus passes fields of rice and corn as well as palm trees and ancient Kapok trees, which look like the vegetative equivalent of body builders, flexing their broad limbs, striking impressive profiles.

Up in the front of the bus, Kellie is talking to her boys who are clearly tired from the last few days. She and Scott have decided they should see humanity at its best and worst, both of which are in stark relief here. Kellie is speaking to them, to everyone within earshot, but probably mostly to herself:

> Looking at the faces of the homeless and the poor and the suffering, it was the same experience I had when I looked into the monstrance. I saw Jesus in them. I yearned to be with them. I yearned to join them in their sufferings, to inspire them, and encourage them.

And then this:

> The greatest poverty I have ever seen is someone who does not believe in God.

And then this:

> People ask me frequently, "Isn't your ministry clothes?" I usually laugh and respond, "Our ministry

is to share the love of God and His mercy worldwide. The clothes, the food, the shoes are just actions of that mercy." What good is it to give away clothes or food to others, if they lose their souls? How much will it profit a child to have new shoes if you don't share with him that God will clothe him for eternity?

And further this:

Eternal life is worth fighting for.

And finally this:

All my life, I've felt compassion for people who suffer. I want them to know they are not alone.

Making their way through the red dirt streets of Yamoussoukro, the Missionaries pull into Our Lady of the Visitation where students have assembled wearing shirts that bear their parish's name. They are singing with accompaniment from an organ and drums. A delegation of priests and politicians, including the pastor of the parish, Fr. Jacques Kowassi, greets the Missionaries as they step off the bus. The Missionaries are ushered into the open-air church. It wasn't intended to be open-air. It's unfinished. The parish doesn't have the funds to finish it. But it serves as shelter for now, a place of refuge from the weather. The place is packed.

Before Holy Mass, Kellie is invited to speak. As a gift to the parish, she presents a large image of the Divine Mercy. Some young men of the parish carry it out and set it in front of the tabernacle. Kellie explains how the image was given to St. Faustina and that Jesus promises many graces to those who meditate on the image. "In Jesus' eyes, you can see His compassion. In His hands, you can see the wounds He bore for us," she says. "From His Heart, you can see the rays that represent Blood and Water. The Blood represents the sacrifice of the Eucharist, the Precious Blood of Christ. The pale ray represents Baptism and the forgiveness of sins," she says. "This image is an image of action, an action of tenderness and compassion. Through this image, Jesus is saying, 'Return to Me.' This is a God who wants to give us mercy and to forgive us for our sins. And just in case the image isn't enough, He put what He wants us to say to Him underneath: 'Jesus, I trust in You.'"

For the next five minutes, she has the entire congregation chanting, "Jesus, I trust in You" in their native French. Their voices are powerful. The place is on the verge of erupting. Father Jacques is hoping the rafters don't cave in even as he himself claps enthusiastically.

"God loves you and, through us, He brought this image to your village to let you know that He loves you and hears every utterance of prayer you make," Kellie is saying above the chants. "Imitate our Savior. Pray for people who hurt you, who persecute you. Mercy is a verb. Mercy is actively relieving the suffering of others and helping them carry their cross."

After Mass, the Missionaries hand out Divine Mercy prayercards. Hundreds of them. People swarm to receive them. Children marvel at them. They kiss the image. Even as the bus starts to pull away, arms reach to the windows as Kellie is handing out piles of prayercards, like shoveling coal to keep a fire burning.

"We need more prayercards!" Kellie calls to her fellow Missionaries. She's hanging out the bus window. Someone hands her a huge stack that she puts into outstretched hands.

"Wow," she says, as she takes a seat. "That was incredible."

Everyone is quiet now as the bus pulls through the city center and back onto the highway and then back into the countryside.

Kellie breaks the silence. Self-effacing is one of her stronger characteristics, and she's admitting she feels a little funny that she just led what amounted to a sweaty, religious revival, the sort made famous by Baptists in the South.

"The point is," she says, "my prayer is that people will forget my name and remember the image of the Divine Mercy."

Back in Manassas a couple months later, the House of Mercy is filling with impoverished people on a Saturday morning. They are picking up clothing and food. Kellie has been making lots of calls lately to benefactors, telling them about Cote d'Ivoire and about the increasing needs of the poor in northern Virginia.

Whatever happens, Kellie knows this: "The Chaplet of Divine Mercy is the link that will always bind the House of Mercy to the people of Cote d'Ivoire," she says. "One day, we pray we will see each other in heaven. For now, they will always be a part of our ministry, in our hearts and prayers."

She's attaching a Divine Mercy prayercard to a used winter coat. What a deal: accepting Jesus' mercy. That's the only price you have to pay to stay warm in the coming winter.

Postscript:

Today, the House of Mercy continues to pray for the citizens of Cote d'Ivoire. However, due to financial constraints, they are no longer able to perform missionary work there. The House of Mercy has since moved into a new 16,000-square-foot facility in Manassas and feeds thousands of children, not only in northern Virginia but in developing countries around the world. In addition, the House of Mercy has expanded its thrift store to the general public. It continues to provide free clothing, new shoes, and classes for the poor that focus on financial independence and education. Visitors to the House of Mercy can spend time in reflection at the indoor Grotto of Lourdes, pray for the intentions of others, or join in to help serve.

To contact the House of Mercy
Website: divinemercynow.org
Phone: 703-659-1636

Mailing address:
8170 Flannery Court
Manassas, VA 20109

Felix Carroll

CHAPTER 17

Eric Mahl

'Freely You Received, Freely Give'

O my Jesus, each of Your saints reflects one of Your virtues; I desire to reflect Your compassionate Heart, full of mercy; I want to glorify it. Let Your mercy, O Jesus, be impressed upon my Heart and soul like a seal, and this will be my badge in this and the future life.

— Diary of St. Faustina, 1242

Be the hammer, not the nail!
Be the hammer, not the nail!

When a college football coach of his would bark that mantra, Eric Mahl would nod, slap his hands together, take to the field, and then pound the opposition into submission. He was a star linebacker, all muscle and sinew and intensity as he cut fearlessly through an offensive line and onto sports pages throughout Ohio.

In his senior year at Kent State University, he was a hammer picked up by the National Football League, signed as a free agent to the Cleveland Browns. This was a dream come true, of course. But when he first emerged from the tunnel and onto the field of Cleveland Browns Stadium during the 2005 pre-season, none of the 73,000 cheering fans could possibly imagine what was going on in the mind of this hammer they had read about in rookie reports. Eric could hardly believe it himself. But none of it felt right. After all those years of training and fantasizing, he didn't want to be there. He didn't want to play this game anymore. He didn't want to be the star or the center of attention.

He didn't want to be the hammer. He wanted to be the nail.

✝

Plowing the sidewalks in this part of town doesn't seem to be anyone's priority. But few pedestrians venture out in weather like this anyway. Not unless they have to. Not unless they're Eric Mahl. He chooses to. Here he is, on the west side of Cleveland on a cold, snowy February day in 2013, finding his footing in the slush, the water seeping through his shoes, and the daylight yielding to darkness.

He may very well be Cleveland's happiest, homeless person. They don't quite know what to make of him around these parts. He started showing up a few months back. For starters, he's one of the few Caucasians. At 29 years of age, he's certainly one of the youngest men waiting in line at the soup kitchens or blowing the steam off a free cup of coffee on the corner, or bedding down in a homeless shelter. Some sneer at him, figuring he's an undercover cop in these neighborhoods that have seen better days. Others simply ignore him because they ignore everyone. Still others find him too curious of a creature to not examine more closely.

He's different. That's for sure. He makes eye contact. He speaks of God. He's got Hollywood good looks. He smiles a lot, yet doesn't seem to be mentally disturbed.

He's certainly different in ways they can't imagine. He lives among people who have lost everything. Eric didn't lose everything; he gave it away. All of it. He was a professional football player in that huge, glittering stadium just across the river, but no one here knows about that. He has no intention of telling them either. He certainly doesn't look like a football player anymore. That was eight years and 60 pounds ago. He has allowed all those fibers in all those muscles to disappear down to normal size.

When he vowed to God several years back that he would become "little," he didn't mean it quite so literally, but he's certain God has a sense of humor. That was made clear to him a few weeks back when he was plodding down the road, his legs aching and his feet burning with blisters when he happened to gaze up and see a billboard with a photo of his old friend and fellow teammate at Kent State and the Cleveland Browns, Josh Cribbs, larger than life — a multi-million dollar superstar cutting a swath through the secondary and selling one thing or another.

"I laughed," says Eric, who has zero regrets for the life he left behind.

He has zero regrets because God gives him constant confirmation that he's doing the right thing. And what exactly is he doing?

Well, meet Lucy.

✝

As she and Eric approach her encampment on a secluded greensward along the banks of the Cuyahoga River, Lucy makes a high-pitched smooching sound that has the effect she's hoping for. From within the natural shelter of pucker brush and plastic tarp steps a litter of kittens she's been caring for. They yawn and make their way toward her in a gentle trot. She's found some discarded food in boxes beside the market just up the hill. Lucy (not her real name) will eat some of the food herself and share the rest with her feline friends.

Eric was introduced to Lucy two weeks ago by a volunteer in a shelter. She now calls Eric a friend.

"Do you see any light in my eyes?" Lucy asked him a couple days ago. She is 60. She has multiple sclerosis. Walking is becoming more and more difficult. Her intestines are being eaten away by Gonorrhea. Bowel movements have become increasingly painful. She won't admit herself into a hospital because they will institutionalize her. She's been through that before and has no intention of allowing that to happen again. Even when raped — which she has been, multiple times — she doesn't bother reporting it to the cops because, she says, they, too, will put her away.

She chooses her tumbledown camp over staying in shelters, even on the coldest of nights, because in some shelters, it's not safe being a woman. She carries a weapon. It's a jagged metal top of a tin can with a section of it folded upon itself that serves as a grip. Someone raided her camp recently and slashed the tarp under which she sleeps. If anyone comes to raid it again, she'll do everything within her power to make sure the person regrets it.

Eric told her that he does, indeed, see light in her eyes. He sees the light of Christ, he told her.

"It's there," he said. "It just needs to be brought out."

While she has all but given up on humanity, remarkably, Lucy believes in God. She even quotes Scripture, preferring the more unsettling passages from the Book of Revelation. She believes the End Times are upon us. The signs are everywhere to see, she says.

Eric is certain why God has placed Lucy into his life. It's because her understanding of God is so erroneous — dangerous, even. Several days ago, she told him that God has already condemned her for what she's done in her life.

Where did she learn that? There's no telling. But as far as she's concerned, when considering all the grave sins she has committed all these years, how could it be any other way?

Eric has given his entire life to God in order to set the record straight in such matters.

"You have not been condemned," he told her. "There's nothing you have done in your life that can cause Him to turn away from you. He wants you to open your heart to Him, to love Him, and trust in Him and turn to Him with all of your pain and fears. We have until our very last breath to be saved."

Eric isn't sure Lucy believes him. She's dying, and they both know it. She's a prime example for why giving up wealth and renown isn't as crazy as it sounds.

Time was he could bench press 450 pounds and squat 700-and-something pounds. That's an absurd amount of weight. Eric set records in high school and in college. In retrospect, that he trained day in and day out for years on end in order to accomplish such feats probably is the single craziest thing he's ever done.

Born and raised to a loving, supportive family in Monroeville, Ohio, a tiny town surrounded by farms and woods, Eric recalls that as a boy he led a prayerful life and had an intimate relationship with God. By middle school, however, athletics eclipsed his spiritual life. Everyone could see he had natural abilities in sports. He became obsessed with being the best — the fastest, toughest, and even the handsomest. He was superlative on all counts. The girls loved him. The record books yielded to him.

By the time Kent State University offered him a full scholarship to play football, he was a hometown hero. He lived up to expectations in college, becoming team captain and being named all-conference.

During senior year, for reasons he cannot explain, he felt called to pray the Rosary. One day he wandered into a religious shop called Our Lady's Gifts. The proprietor, a woman in her 70s or 80s, took a liking to Eric. She saw in him a big lug with a big heart. They became the best of friends. She introduced him to the writings of St. Thérèse of Lisieux, known as the "Little Flower," and to St. Faustina Kowalska, known as the "Apostle of Divine Mercy." The woman seemed most excited to share with him the revelations of St. Faustina in the 1930s, which serve to underscore for modern times the Gospel call to turn away from sin, trust in God, and be the face of the Merciful Lord to a broken world.

Eric couldn't help noticing how in her *Diary*, St. Faustina uses the word "poor" almost habitually, mostly in its adjectival form. Saint Faustina writes of her "poor soul," of "poor sinners," her "poor heart," of "poor humans," even of "poor earth." Why *poor*? Because that's the condition of humanity when it's separated from God.

Eric felt a tug at his heart. Maybe he wasn't supposed to be a superstar. Maybe he was to offer himself as an instrument of God, unanchored to possessions and obsessions of the material world. By the time he suited up in a Cleveland Browns uniform in late summer 2005, his heart wasn't in it. When, midway through the season, the New York Jets picked him up with hopes he'd be the heir apparent in a defense whose linebacker positions were up for grabs, he no longer wanted to be the best.

He was relieved when, at the end of the season, the Jets released him. Eric's agent had plans for him. Other teams would be interested in signing him. A place on a roster could have been his if he wanted it. Instead, Eric walked away from it all.

He knew what he wanted — God and whatever God wanted of him — but he didn't have the courage to pursue it yet. He parlayed his notoriety in Cleveland for a business career as a pharmaceutical salesman. He made a six-figure salary. He had a beautiful apartment, a veritable bulwark of tailored suits, and a new car.

But enough was enough. In 2009, he could no longer ignore God's call. He gave it all away — all of his possessions except for a single change of clothes. He brought his suits to the Salvation Army. He gave his savings to local charities. He gave his SUV to his father.

He and his parents went to Mass on the morning he officially became poor. Then, they went to the airport where they shared tears before Eric boarded an airplane heading to Texas. For the next three years, he lived at a desert hermitage. He had wanted to see if he was called to be a monk.

✝

That's what he needed — to immerse himself in the Gospels, to live in silence, solitude, prayer, and penance. There was one thing Eric asked of his superior: that he would be allowed to awake at 3 a.m. each morning to pray the Chaplet of Divine Mercy, an intercessory prayer given to the world through St. Faustina. He would pray the chaplet for the salvation of souls throughout the world.

During those three years, God spoke to his heart through the Gospels. Slowly, God made it clear that this time at the hermitage was merely preparation for a future ministry. Eric had come to know he was not to lead an entirely contemplative life in a hermitage; he was to take the Gospels to the streets. He was not to be a preacher, but rather a living witness of God's mercy to those who long to see the face of Jesus, whether they know it or not.

With the graces of his superior, he left the hermitage at the beginning of 2012 and went back to Ohio where he and his father immediately embarked on a road trip to the National Shrine of The Divine Mercy in Stockbridge, Massachusetts. Eric said he felt a call to visit the Shrine for the Feast of the Presentation of Our Lord, which commemorates the day on which the Child Jesus was brought to the temple to be consecrated to God. He also felt a call to present himself to "Fr. Joseph." He had no idea who "Fr. Joseph" was. He had no idea that "Fr. Joseph" was the honorary title for the director of the Association of Marian Helpers, headquartered on the grounds of the Shrine. The current "Fr.

Joseph" is Fr. Michael Gaitley, MIC. Eric and Fr. Michael met after Mass, and Eric told him of his plans to serve the poor and that he felt drawn to visit the Shrine and speak with "Fr. Joseph." Father Michael listened to Eric's story with amazement but didn't feel he had a clear answer for Eric's discernment. He shared about the works of the Marians and other communities, particularly those who serve the poor. Apart from this, neither of them quite knew what to make of the meeting, but they promised to pray for one another, and Fr. Michael gave him his blessing.

What became clear was that the message of Divine Mercy, of which the Marians are official promoters, was tugging at Eric's heart. He went on pilgrimage to Rome that April to celebrate Divine Mercy Sunday at the Vatican. Before Mass, he was able to go to confession inside St. Peter's, a grace in and of itself. Without knowing Eric's circumstances — his desires to serve the poor and to die to self in order to live for Christ — the priest at the end of confession told him, "You are to love, serve, and be quiet, imitating our Lord Jesus Christ. Go in peace." It served as confirmation for Eric. Then, he visited Assisi, famous as the home of St. Francis who radically followed the call of Jesus by shedding himself of the trappings of wealth in order to serve the poor. While in prayer, Eric received further confirmation of his calling when he decided to open the Bible randomly and point to a passage. His finger landed on the Gospel of Matthew, chapter 10, where Jesus sends out the 12 apostles to evangelize to the world. Jesus says: "Freely you received, freely give" (verse 8).

Those words made him think of his parents most of all — how they had sacrificed so much for him and his sister all those years growing up. A day never went by without him knowing he was loved. He feels an obligation to extend those graces, to love those who have been shown no love.

On the streets of Cleveland now, leaning into a stiff wind as he makes his way over the Detroit Avenue Bridge to find a place to stay for the evening, Eric says he understands why St. Faustina was so meticulous about her use of the word "poor" and its variants.

"I've learned how there are plenty of places to receive shelter, food, and clothing, particularly around here," he says, "but wholehearted love and true friendship are lacking. I've found the greatest poverty is loneliness."

✝

There are others things he has learned, too.

For example, he cannot possibly radiate Christ without Christ dwelling within him in the form of the Holy Eucharist. He attends daily Mass.

He cannot serve the poor without being poor. He mops floors in shelters and soup kitchens. He strikes up conversations with complete strangers.

He's learned he cannot take rejection to heart. Quite often, poor people reject him. His particular brand of optimism can strike a discordant note with some.

"Someday, you'll learn," a world-weary panhandler tells him outside the Cathedral of St. John the Evangelist after Eric offers him bread and prayer. The man doesn't want bread or prayer or any nonsense about God, love, and redemption. He wants money. Only money.

Eric has come to view encounters like this as a kind of grace.

"It's humbling," Eric says. "And it helps me remember how sorrowful Jesus must be because so many people reject Him."

He has learned never to assume he's safe in the streets.

"Someday," a man in the shelter recently told him, "you're going to hear something you wished you didn't hear." Translation: Don't crowd certain people when they're engaged in conversation. It could be a drug deal, and drug dealers don't take kindly to strangers hearing things they shouldn't be hearing.

He has learned that such brokenness only underscores the importance of prayer.

"In the shelters, you hear people screaming and snoring, and you smell the stink, and meanwhile it's difficult for me to sleep, and I might not sleep at all," he says. "But it's an opportunity because I can lay there and pray the Chaplet of Divine Mercy for all of them without them even knowing it." He has learned that Satan has a field day with the destitute. "They've all experienced him," Eric says. "The Devil is real. They'll tell you that. There is such a thing as spiritual warfare."

✝

Eric comes upon a homeless man off Detroit Avenue who seems on the verge of asking for a handout, but he probably sees in Eric a fellow homeless man. Instead, the man, who identifies himself as Michael G., makes a comment about the cold. It's Monday, Feb. 4, 2013. Temperatures are expected to dip to 5 degrees Fahrenheit this evening. Homeless shelters that normally don't open on Mondays are opening tonight.

It's 5 p.m., the sun is setting, and you can feel the cold coming on.

"Go to Malachi tonight," Eric advises the man, referring to the nearby St. Malachi Center. "They have beds and hot food."

"Thanks," Michael says. "I found a place to stay, an abandoned house off Clark. It's got heat."

Michael eyes the butter-knife-sized wooden crucifix Eric wears around his neck.

"That's nice, man," he says. "Really nice."

He shares how he hasn't slept in 24 hours "because the demons were surrounding me last night. They were all around me. I kept praying Psalms 45, Psalms 45, Psalms 45."

Eric has learned many who are poor have more than a cursory knowledge of Scripture.

"Invoke Jesus' name," Eric tells the man. "The Devil can't do anything to you when you speak the name of Jesus."

He prays over the man, asking Jesus to protect him from all harm. Then, he reaches into his bag and hands Michael a few prayercards with the image of Divine Mercy on one side and how to pray the chaplet on the back.

"These were blessed by a holy priest," Eric tells him.

Eric reaches back into his bag and pulls out a wooden rosary and hands it to the man.

"Oh, thank you so much, thank you so much," Michael says. As they part ways, the man stops and asks, "Do you have another rosary you can give me? I want to give one to my son."

Eric gives him another set of rosary beads.

"God bless you," Eric says.

"God bless *you*," Michael says.

God keeps putting people like Michael into his path.

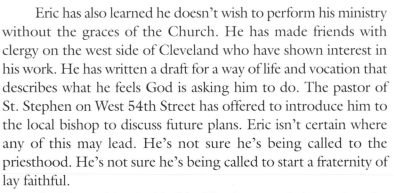

Eric has also learned he doesn't wish to perform his ministry without the graces of the Church. He has made friends with clergy on the west side of Cleveland who have shown interest in his work. He has written a draft for a way of life and vocation that describes what he feels God is asking him to do. The pastor of St. Stephen on West 54th Street has offered to introduce him to the local bishop to discuss future plans. Eric isn't certain where any of this may lead. He's not sure he's being called to the priesthood. He's not sure he's being called to start a fraternity of lay faithful.

God is working in his life. The hammer is becoming the nail, as he seeks God's will for his life. He's sure of that. He feels certain God wants him to continue devoting his life to serving the poor through the message of Divine Mercy.

Lucy wants to see the graffiti. She hasn't ridden the subway in years, but when she used to, she would marvel at the graffiti covering all those bridge abutments and jersey barriers and brick backsides of old steel mills. It was the work of *artists*, she insists, not "vandals."

The Cleveland skyline to the east is steaming like a shower stall. Eric has scraped together enough change to buy subway tickets on the Red Line, so that Lucy can get a look at what the graffiti artists have been up to all these years. But as the train barrels along, graffiti is nowhere to be seen. The city has cleaned it up. She's disappointed, but she looks on the bright side. It's warm in this train, and she has companionship.

As the train rocks back and forth through a canyon of concrete with no graffiti, Lucy shares a dream she has. She dreams of opening a house for the poor. Not a big house. Maybe for 15 or so. And *only* women. Definitely, only women. The house would include a vegetable garden out back. The women would receive the necessities, she says, and the necessities would not only include food, clothing, and shelter but also spiritual education.

"People need to know about God," Lucy says.

"They do," Eric agrees. "Amen. And they need to know that the greater the sinner, the more right they have to Jesus' mercy. That's what Jesus wants us to know — that it's never too late."

He's trying to convince her.

Lucy nods.

She tells about how she left home in Cleveland at the age of 16 because her father would brutally beat her and her younger brothers. Among the many regrets she lives with is not having taken her brothers with her.

"I didn't do right by them," she says.

From there, she wandered the country, from California to Florida, living as a hippie. They were good times, she says. Then, they turned into bad times.

She came back home to Cleveland in recent years because this is her home. This is where she wants to die. She knows all its parks, all its fountains, and all its statues. Like Eric, she's proud of this city even as she looks upon its downtown from under a tarp she calls home, built into the banks of the Cuyahoga River.

From her camp, you can just make out the tippy-top of Cleveland Browns Stadium, a mile to the northeast and a world away.

Postscript:

The meeting Eric had with Fr. Michael in 2012 has proved providential after all. Just before the printing of this book, Eric found an old, framed image of the Merciful Jesus in a shop during a visit home with his parents. He felt called again to travel to the National Shrine of The Divine Mercy in Stockbridge for the Feast of the Presentation of Our Lord on February 2, 2013. Again, he felt called to speak with "Fr. Joseph," but this time Eric wanted to present him with the image he had found. Eric met with Fr. Michael and again shared with him his work in the streets and how it seems to tie in so well with the message of Divine Mercy. He also shared about how he had looked into other communities, and how they didn't seem to be the right fit for him. Hearing this, and seeing that the Lord had called Eric back to the Shrine, Fr. Michael suggested that maybe the Lord might be calling him to work with the Marians to spread Divine Mercy, particularly to the poor.

This suggestion resonated with Eric, and the two men explored the idea with the Marians' Provincial Superior in the United States and Argentina, Fr. Kazimierz Chwalek, MIC, on February 2. Thoroughly impressed by Eric's sincerity, Fr. Kaz formally invited him to spend a period of time in Stockbridge being formed in the Divine Mercy message and devotion, working with the region's poor, and helping the Marians with a new initiative to make affordable canvas images of the Divine Mercy. Eric particularly loved this last point, because for many years, he had felt that his vocation could really be summed up in the idea of St. Faustina, namely, of being transformed into the Lord's mercy (see *Diary*, 163), of being a kind of "image" of Divine Mercy for the poor.

Eric now lives and works with the Marian community in Stockbridge.

The hammer is becoming the nail.

ABOUT THE AUTHOR

Felix Carroll has twice been named *Writer of the Year* by the New York Press Association. He's won Best Feature Writing and Best Environmental Writing awards from the National Newspaper Association and New York Press Association; Best Enterprise Writing from the New England Press Association; and several writing awards from the Catholic Press Association.

He serves as editor of thedivinemercy.org and marian.org for the Marian Fathers of the Immaculate Conception in Stockbridge, Massachusetts. He's a feature writer and photographer for Marian Helper magazine. He's a columnist for the *Albany Times-Union* and the *Cape Cod Times*. His work has appeared in the *Boston Globe, Houston Chronicle, Seattle Post-Intelligencer, Dallas Morning News*, and *Chicago Sun-Times*.

He lives in Monterey, Massachusetts, with his wife and son.

PROMOTING DIVINE MERCY SINCE 1941

Marian Press, the publishing apostolate of the Marian Fathers of the Immaculate Conception of the B.V.M., has published and distributed millions of religious books, magazines, and pamphlets that teach, encourage, and edify Catholics around the world. Our publications promote and support the ministry and spirituality of the Marians worldwide. Loyal to the Holy Father and to the teachings of the Catholic Church, the Marians fulfill their special mission by:

- Fostering devotion to Mary, the Immaculate Conception.

- Promoting The Divine Mercy message and devotion.

- Offering assistance to the dying and the deceased, especially the victims of war and disease.

- Promoting Christian knowledge, administering parishes, shrines, and conducting missions.

Based in Stockbridge, Mass., Marian Press is known as the publisher of the *Diary of Saint Maria Faustina Kowalska*, and the Marians are the leading authorities on the Divine Mercy message and devotion.

Stockbridge is also the home of the National Shrine of The Divine Mercy, the Association of Marian Helpers, and a destination for thousands of pilgrims each year.

Globally, the Marians' ministries also include missions in developing countries where the spiritual and material needs are enormous.

To learn more about the Marians, their spirituality, publications or ministries, visit **marian.org** or **thedivinemercy.org**, the Marians' website that is devoted exclusively to Divine Mercy.

Below is a view of the National Shrine of The Divine Mercy and its Residence in Stockbridge, Massachusetts. The Shrine, which was built in the 1950s, was declared a National Shrine by the National Conference of Catholic Bishops on March 20, 1996.

© MARIE ROMAGNANO

Visit us at the National Shrine of The Divine Mercy in Stockbridge, Mass.
For more information: thedivinemercy.org/shrine or 413-298-1118.

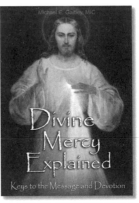

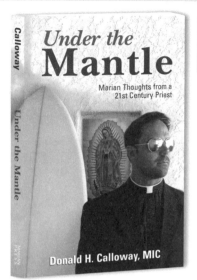
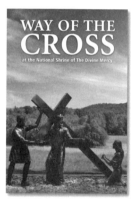
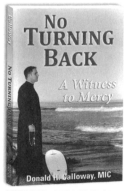

YOUR ESSENTIAL DIVINE MERCY RESOURCE

DIARY OF SAINT MARIA FAUSTINA KOWALSKA: DIVINE MERCY IN MY SOUL

The *Diary* chronicles the message that Jesus, the Divine Mercy, gave to the world through this humble nun. In it, we are reminded to trust in His forgiveness — and as Christ is merciful, so, too, are we instructed to be merciful to others. Written in the 1930s, the *Diary* exemplifies God's love toward mankind and to this day, remains a source of hope and renewal. Keep the *Diary* next to your Bible for constant insight and inspiration for your spiritual growth!

LARGE PAPERBACK:
NBFD 9780944203040
768 pages, including 24 pages
of color photographs, 5 ½" x 7 ¾".

COMPACT PAPERBACK:
DNBF 9781596141100
768 pages, including 24 pages of black
and white photographs, 4" x 7".

AUDIO DIARY OF ST. FAUSTINA
Includes all passages from the printed
Diary, prayerful music, and three ren-
ditions of the Chaplet of the Divine
Mercy. 33 hours on 27 CDs.
ADCD 9781596142299

**DELUXE LEATHER-BOUND
EDITION**
Treasure this handsome, Deluxe
Leather Edition for years to come.
Includes a special dedication from
the Marians of the Immaculate
Conception in commemoration of
the first World Apostolic Congress
on Mercy, gilded edges, a ribbon
marker, and 20 pages of color
photographs. 768 pages, 4 ⅜" x 7 ⅛".

BURGUNDY:
DDBURG 9781596141896
NAVY BLUE:
DDBLUE 9781596141902

For our complete line of books, prayercards, pamphlets, rosaries, and chaplets visit
TheDivineMercy.org or call 1-800-462-7426 to have our latest catalog sent to you.